DICTIONARY 3

Compiled and Edited by

AMY BROWN

JOHN DOWNING

JOHN SCEATS

PYRAMID PRIMARY DICTIONARY SERIES

Published by

PYRAMID PUBLICATIONS

PYRAMID PRIMARY DICTIONARY THREE

Copyright © 1972 by A. L. Brown, J. A. Downing and J. Sceats
Published in cooperation with W. & R. Chambers Ltd.

ISBN 0-515-02698-0

Library of Congress Catalog Card Number: 71-152246

First Printing March, 1972

Printed in the United States of America

Illustrations by Sostres

Cover design by Larry Lurin

PYRAMID PUBLICATIONS
NEW YORK, NEW YORK

Preface

About this book

A dictionary is a list of words we can use. There
are many different kinds of dictionaries, some of
them very easy and some much more difficult. This
one is the third of a graded series of four dictionaries
for children. If you find it is too difficult, use
Dictionary Two. If you are quite used to dictionaries,
and this one does not have all the words you want,
then go on to *Dictionary Four*.

The job of a dictionary is to tell us about words.
A large dictionary for adults contains all the words
people ever use and all their different meanings. It
may also tell us where words come from and how
they are pronounced. But the main use of any
dictionary—and of this one—is to tell us what a
word means if we don't know it, and how to spell it
correctly.

The words in dictionaries are always arranged in
alphabetical order, which means that there is only
one right place for each word. You should be able to
find the word you want very quickly, even in a large
dictionary. If you are not good at this it is better to
practice first on *Dictionaries One* and *Two*, until
you are quick and sure.

How to find a word

Suppose you come across a word like **octopus** and
want to know what it means. You know that **o**
comes somewhere near the middle of the alphabet,
so open the dictionary at the middle. You may be
lucky and find **o** the first time. But if you find that
all the words begin with **l** or **p** you have to ask
yourself if **o** comes before or after. You will soon
get very good at this.

Then look at the second letter of **octopus**, and find the words beginning **oc-**. Then, if you look at the third letter, you know that **octopus** comes after **ocean**, because **t** comes after **e**.

The letters above the line on the tops of the pages are the beginnings of the first and last words on those pages; they will save you looking through a lot of words before you have found the right page.

When you have found your word

After each word comes an explanation of what the word most often means. Sometimes there is a picture to help. Many words have quite a lot of different meanings, so test whether the one which is given makes sense in the sentence where you found the word. If it does not make sense at all there may be another meaning for the word which you could find in *Dictionary Four*.

If you don't understand some of the words used in the explanation, look them up too; you will find them in this dictionary.

It is sometimes interesting to look up words that you already know, to see if you agree with how the meaning is explained.

Are there any words in this Preface that you are not sure about? Why not try looking them up now?

To parents and teachers

Guidance on how best to use *Pyramid Primary Dictionaries* with children will be found in *Words Children Want to Use*, the handbook to the series, which also contains an account of the research on which the series is based.

abacus a frame with beads on rods, used for counting

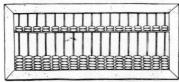

abandon to go away forever from something or somebody. The same word also means to stop what you are doing before you have finished it.

abbess a woman who is the head of the nuns in a convent or abbey

abbey a monastery or a convent; the big church of a monastery or convent

abbot a man who is the head of the monks in a monastery or abbey

abbreviation a short way of writing or printing a word, such as Dr. for Doctor, Jan. for January

abdomen the lower part of the body which contains the stomach

ability strength, cleverness or skill

able having the strength, cleverness or skill to do something

abolish to get rid of or to put an end to something

above higher than; over

abroad away in another country

abrupt sudden; hurried

absent missing; away; not present

abundant more than enough; in great plenty

accent   tone of voice; a way of pronouncing words

accept   to agree to receive something

accident   something that happens by chance, usually unpleasant

account   a statement of money owing or spent. The same word also means an explanation.

accurate   correct; exactly right

accuse   to say someone has done something wrong

ace   a card, domino or die with one spot or mark

ache   a dull pain that goes on and on

acid   a liquid which can burn your skin. The same word also means tasting sour or sharp.

acorn   the nut or seed that grows on an oak tree

acrobat   a person who does clever tricks, like balancing on a rope at a circus

across   from one side to the other side of something

act   anything which is done is an act. The same word also means to pretend you are someone other than yourself, as in a play or film.

actor   a man or boy who acts in a play or film

action   something done; a series of acts performed

active   doing something; being busy or lively

actress   a woman or girl who acts in a play or film

actual   real; not imaginary

add   to put something together with something else. You add two and two to make four ($2 + 2 = 4$).

addition   something added; the act of adding

additional   extra; added to something

address   the name and number of your house and the street and town where you are living. The same word also means to write or speak to people.

adenoids   two small fleshy lumps at the back of the nose

admiral   a very important officer in the navy

admire   to think very well of someone or something

admit   to agree that something is so. The same word means to allow someone to come in.

adult   a person who is fully grown up

advance   to move forward

adventure   an exciting or dangerous thing that you do or that happens to you

aerial   the metal rods or wires which receive or send radio or television signals

affair   a happening or an event

affect   to do something that causes a change

affection   great liking; fondness

afford   to have enough money for something you want to buy

afloat   floating on the water

afraid   frightened; full of fear

after   later; behind

afternoon   the time between midday and sunset

afterwards   at a later time

again   once more

against   in an opposite direction to; on the opposite side of

age   the number of years something or someone has been alive, or has existed

agile   lively; nimble

agree   to consent to something, or to think the same as someone else

agreeable   friendly; easy to get on with

aground   stuck on the sand or rocks. When ships run aground they cannot move without help.

ahead   in front: before

aim   to point a gun or other weapon steadily at the thing you want to hit

air   the mixture of gases which we breathe and which surrounds the earth

aircraft   any machine that can rise in the air and move through it

air force   the aviation section of a country's armed forces, such as the United States Air Force

airgun   a gun in which the bullet is shot by the force of compressed air

airman   a man who flies or helps to fly aircraft

airplane   a flying machine

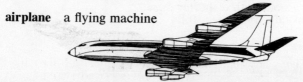

airport the place where airplanes come in to land and take off

airtight closed so tightly that air cannot get in or out

aisle a pathway between rows of seats in a church or a theater

alarm sudden surprise or fear. The same word also means a warning of danger, often a bell.

album a book of blank pages in which you keep a collection of things like stamps or photographs

ale a kind of beer

alert wide awake; active or watchful

algebra a branch of mathematics in which you use letters as well as figures

alibi an excuse by someone that he could not have done something, because he can prove that he was somewhere else when it happened

alight in flames; burning

alive living; not dead

all the whole of; everything or everyone

alley a narrow passage between buildings in cities and towns

alligator a dangerous animal much like a crocodile, but with a shorter nose

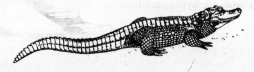

allow   to permit or let

alloy   a mixture of two or more metals

all right   good; safe and sound; agreed

almanac   a book that gives information about the weather and other things that may happen in the days, weeks and months of one year

almond   a kind of flat nut that grows inside the fruit of an almond tree

almost   nearly, but not quite

alone   all by yourself; with nobody else

aloud   out loud; the opposite of silent

alphabet   all the letters used in a language, arranged in a special order

already   sooner than expected

alsatian   a large wolf-like dog

also   as well as; too; in addition

altar   a kind of raised table inside a church

alter   to make a change in something, to make or become different in some way

alteration   a change

although   even if; but; in spite of

aluminum   a lightweight, silver-colored metal

always   at all times; forever

amateur   someone who plays games or takes part in something without being paid, because he likes doing it

amaze   to surprise greatly

ambition   a wish to do very well, or to have power

amble   to walk along slowly

ambulance   a special car for taking people who are ill or hurt to the hospital

among   in the midst of

amount   a quantity; the sum reached when several things are added together

ample   of a large size; in plenty

amuse   to make others smile or laugh by something you say or do

anchor   a heavy iron hook which is attached to a ship by a chain. When it is thrown over the side, it digs into the sea bed and stops the ship from moving.

angel   a messenger from God

angle   the corner made when two lines meet at a point

angora   wool made from the long silky hair of the angora goat or rabbit

angry   very cross; in a bad temper

animal   any living creature which is not a plant

ankle   the thin bony part of your leg just above your foot

anniversary   a day which is remembered each year for something special which happened once, like a wedding anniversary

announce   to make something known by telling everyone

annoy   to make someone rather cross

anorak   a waterproof jacket, usually with a hood

another   one more; a different one

answer   anything said or written in reply, usually to a question

ant   a small insect

antarctic   at or around the South Pole

anthem   the national song of a country. The same word also means a piece of music sung by a church choir.

anvil   an iron block on which pieces of metal can be hammered into shape

anxiety   worry; a feeling of fear about something you think might happen

anxious   worried or afraid about something you think might happen

anything   a thing of any kind

apart   not together

apartment   a home on one floor which is part of a larger building

ape   a large monkey without a tail

apex   the highest tip of something, such as the top point of a triangle

apparatus   a collection of things that help you to do something, such as ropes and bars in a gymnasium

appeal   to ask for help

appear   to come into sight

appearance   the way someone or something looks to you; the coming into sight of someone or something

appetite   the desire to eat

applaud   to show you like some entertainment or performance by clapping your hands together

apple   a round red, green or yellow fruit which grows on a tree

approach   to go nearer to someone or something

approximate   nearly correct

apricot   a fruit which looks like a small yellow peach

apron   a piece of cloth which you tie around you to keep your clothes clean

aquarium   a container, usually a glass tank, where fish and other water animals are kept for people to look at

arc   a part of a circle, a curved line

arch   a part of something, usually a building, that is curved, such as the top of a doorway or window

archery   shooting at a target with bow and arrow

architect   someone who designs and plans
     buildings

arclight   a lamp lit by an arc of electricity

arctic   at or around the North Pole;
     very cold

area   the extent of space on the ground or on
     a floor

arena   a large open space with seats all around,
     where you can watch games or sports

argue   to give reasons for or against something
     which is being discussed

argument   reasons for or against your opinion about
     something; a discussion

arise   to get up

arithmetic   working with numbers, like adding,
     subtracting, multiplying and dividing

arm   the part of your body between your hand
     and your shoulder

armada   a great fleet of warships

armadillo   a small animal with an armor-like
     covering

armchair   a chair with sides on which to rest your
     arms

armor   a covering, usually made of metal, to
     protect the body in battle

armpit   the hollow place under the top part of your
     arm

arms   war weapons, such as guns and cannons

army   a large group of soldiers

around   on all sides

arouse   to wake someone or stir him into action

arrange   to put in a special order

arrive   to reach the place you set out for

arrow   a thin straight stick made of wood with a sharp pointed tip. You shoot it with a bow.

art   drawing, painting and sculpture. The same word is also used when something is done with great skill.

artful   cunning; clever in a rather sneaky way

article   a thing of a particular kind, such as an article of clothing. The same word also means a piece written in a newspaper or magazine.

artist   a person who paints or draws pictures

ascend   to go up; to move upward

ash   the powdery stuff left when something has completely burned up

ashamed   feeling shame

aside   to one side; apart

ask   to put a question to someone

asleep   sleeping; not awake

aspirin   a pain-killing medicine, usually in white tablets

ass   a donkey, an animal rather like a small horse

assemble   to meet together, as when the whole
school is called together for assembly

assist   to help

assistant   a helper

assorted   of many different kinds

astrologer   a fortune-teller who studies the stars

astrology   the study of the stars as a way of telling
your fortune

astronaut   someone who travels
in space

astronomer   a scientist who studies the stars and
other bodies in the sky

astronomy   the scientific study of stars and other
bodies in the sky

athlete   someone who is good at sports and games

atlas   a book of maps

atmosphere   the air that is around the earth

atom   an extremely small particle of anything

attach   to fasten, join or tie together

attack   to make a move to hurt someone or
something

attempt   to try; to make an effort

attend   to be present. The same word also means
to listen carefully to someone.

attendant   a helper in a public place, such as a museum or movie theater

attic   a room just under the roof of a building

attract   to make something or someone come nearer

attractive   charming; lovely; having the power to make people want to be near you

auction   a public sale where things are sold to the people who offer the most money for them

audience   a group of people listening to or watching something like a play or a concert

aunt   the sister of your father or mother

authority   the power to control what other people do. The principal of a school has authority over the teachers and pupils.

autobiography   the story of a person's life written by himself and not by someone else

automobile   any vehicle with an engine, meant to be driven on the road

autumn   the season between summer and winter, when the leaves fall

avenue   a wide street or pathway, usually with trees on both sides

aviation   the art of flying aircraft

aviator   a pilot who flies an aircraft

avoid   to escape; to keep out of the way of something

await   to wait for or look for

awake   not asleep. You can hear and see what is going on around you.

award   to give someone something he has won, like a prize or medal

aware   knowing about something, as when you are aware of the danger of crossing a road with heavy traffic

away   not here or with you; absent

awe   great fear and wonder; great respect

awful   very bad, ugly or nasty

awkward   clumsy. The same word also means not convenient or not comfortable.

ax   a sharp tool with a long handle, used for chopping wood

axis   a real or imaginary line through the middle of an object, around which the object turns

axle   the long bar on a vehicle to which the wheels are attached

azalea   a shrub like a rhododendron, but smaller, with brightly colored flowers

azure   a clear sky-blue color

babble   to talk or make sounds in a foolish way: to make a murmuring sound as water does in a stream or brook

baboon   a large monkey with a short tail and a long dog-like face

baby   an infant; a very young child

babyish   like a baby

bachelor   a man who has not married

bacon   pigmeat that has been dried and salted

bad   not good; wrong; spoiled

badge   a special sign or mark you wear to show you belong to a certain organization

badger   a gray, black and white striped animal which burrows in the earth with its long front claws

badminton   a game rather like tennis, in which you use a smaller racket and a shuttlecock

baffling   too hard or puzzling to understand

bag   a sack for holding things, often made of paper or plastic, but sometimes of leather or cloth

baggage   another word for luggage

bait   food used to attract fish or animals, so that they can be caught

bake   to cook in an oven

baker   a person who bakes and sells bread and cakes

balance   to hold something steady so that it does not tip or fall over

balcony   a platform, usually with railings or a low wall around it. It is built out from the side of a building.

bald   without any hair on the head

bale   a specially packed bundle of something, like straw or cotton

ball   an object which is completely round, often used for playing games. The same word also means a splendid dancing party.

ballerina   a girl ballet dancer

ballet (*say balay*)   a kind of dancing which tells a story in movement, with music, but without using words

balloon   a bag filled with air or gas so that it can float above the ground

ballpoint   a pen with a tiny ball instead of a point at the end

ballroom   a very big room used for dancing

bamboo   a kind of very tall grass with stiff hollow stems which are used for canes or for making furniture

ban   an order to put a stop to something

banana   a long fruit with a thick yellow skin

band   a group of people, sometimes playing musical instruments

bandage   a piece of cloth for covering up a wound

bandit   a robber, usually one who robs people on the roads while they are traveling

bang   a loud and sudden noise. The same word also means to hit something hard.

bangle   a bracelet in the shape of a large ring

banister   a rail to hold on to at the side of a
staircase

banjo   a musical instrument which you play by
plucking the strings

bank   a place where people put their money
so that it will be safe

banknotes   paper money

banner   a flag, sometimes with two poles

banquet   a feast; a special dinner party

bar   a long shaped piece of hard material, usually
metal or wood. The same word also means
a counter where you can buy drinks.

barbecue   an outdoor party where meat is cooked
over an open fire

barbed wire   wire twisted so that sharp points stick
out. It is used as fencing.

barber   a man who cuts hair and shaves beards

bare   without covering or decoration

bargain   something you buy that costs less than the
usual price. The same word also means to
argue with the seller about the price of
something you want to buy.

barge   a cargo boat which has a flat bottom

bark   the tough covering on a tree trunk and
branches. The same word also means the loud
sharp noise dogs and some other animals make.

barley   a plant from which we get a kind of grain; the name of that grain

barn   a large farm building used mainly for storing grain, hay and other crops

barracks   the buildings where soldiers live

barrel   a container made of curved pieces of wood held together with hoops

barren   not able to produce fruit, plants, babies or seeds. The land in deserts and on some mountains is barren because nothing will grow there.

barrier   something, like a fence or wall, that stops you from going further

base   the bottom of anything; the part on which something stands or is built

baseball   a game played with a bat and a ball by two teams of nine players each

basement   the lowest part of a building, usually below the ground

bash   to hit something so hard that it is smashed or dented

bashful   another word for shy

basin   a round bowl for holding water

bask   to warm yourself in the sun

basket   a container made of straw or thin pieces of wood. It has a handle so that you can carry things inside.

bat   a shaped piece of wood used to hit a ball in games. The same word also means a small mouse-like animal that flies at night.

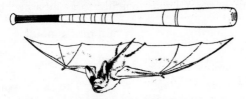

bath   a large container in which you can wash yourself all over

bathe   to take a bath or a swim

bathroom   a room with a bath in it

baton   a stick for beating time to music

batter   to beat or strike something over and over again. The same word also means a mixture of flour and liquid used in cooking.

battery   a container for storing electricity

battle   a fight

battleship   a warship with heavy armor and big guns

bawl   to cry out or shout very loudly

bay   a part of the sea or lake that makes a curve into the land

bayonet   a long sharp blade attached to a rifle, so that it can be used like a spear

bazaar   a market-place or fair where things are sold, usually to raise money for charity

beach   the strip of land next to the sea, covered with sand or pebbles

beacon a signaling light, like a bonfire or lighthouse

bead a small ball with a hole through it. You can thread many beads together to make a necklace.

beak the hard pointed part of a bird's mouth

beaker a tall cup, often without a handle

beam a long thick piece of wood. The same word also means a ray of light.

bean a vegetable with large seeds that grow in pods

bear a large heavy animal with thick shaggy fur and a very short tail. The same word also means to carry something or to put up with something.

beard the hair on a man's chin

bearing the part of a machine on which another part moves or slides. The same word also means the way you carry yourself.

beast an animal

beat to hit over and over again; to keep regular time in music. The same word also means to do better than another person or team in a game or a race.

beautiful lovely; very pretty

beauty great loveliness

become to grow to be something

bed a soft place to sleep, with blankets and a pillow. The same word is also used for a place where flowers are grown, and for the bottom of the sea.

bedclothes   the covers on a bed

bedroom   a room where there is a bed

bedside   the space next to a bed

bedspread   the top cover on a bed

bee   an insect with four wings and a sting. It makes honey and wax.

beech   a kind of tree with smooth silver-gray bark

beef   the meat from a cow or bull

beehive   a house for bees

bee-line   a straight line between two places

beer   a strong drink made from malt

beet   a dark red vegetable

beetle   an insect with four wings. The two front wings are hard, and protect the back wings when they are folded.

before   ahead; in front

beg   to ask earnestly or humbly for something

beggar   someone who lives by asking for money and food from others

begin   to start

beginning   the start of something

behave   to act in a good or a bad way, showing good or bad behavior

behavior   how you act or behave; your manners

behind   at the back of; to the rear of

believe   to accept what someone says as the truth; to have faith

bell   a cup-shaped piece of metal which makes a ringing sound when struck

bellow   to roar or yell loudly

belly   another word for stomach

belong   to be the property of; to be part of

below   underneath; at a lower level

belt   a long strip of material, usually leather, which fastens around the waist

bench   a long seat, usually made of wood

bend   to make something crooked or curved

beneath   under something

beret (*say berray*)   a round flat soft hat

berry   any small round juicy fruit without a pit

berth   a bed or bunk in a ship or train

beside   near; next to

best   most good

bet   to risk your money against someone else's on the result of a game or race

betray   to give away secret information; to let someone down by breaking a promise

better   more than good. The same word also means more clever or skilful than someone else.

between   in a space; among

beware   to be very careful about something that may be dangerous, like a fierce dog or railroad tracks

bewilder   to puzzle someone or make him not sure what to do

beyond   farther on, or farther away

bib   a cloth tied around a baby's neck, to stop food getting on his clothes

bible   a holy book

bicycle   a two-wheeled vehicle with a saddle

bid   to command or invite: to make an offer

big   large; important

bike   a short word for bicycle

bill   a written note of how much money is owing for work which has been done, or for something which has been bought. The same word also means a bird's beak.

billiards   a game played with hard balls and long sticks called cues, on a table covered with thick green cloth

billy-goat   a male goat

bin   a container for corn, bread, coal, or rubbish

bind   to fasten or tie together

binoculars   a kind of double telescope with tubes for both eyes

birch   a tree with smooth silvery or white bark

bird   a winged animal covered with feathers

birdcage   a small cage for a pet bird

birth   coming into life, being born

birthday   the day of the year when you were born

biscuit   a crisp flat cake

bisect   to divide in two equal parts

bit   a small piece of something

bitch   a female dog

bite   to take a piece out of something with your teeth

bitter   tasting sharp and sour; not sweet or sugary

black   the darkest color of all. Coal is black.

blackberry   a small juicy black fruit which grows wild

blackbird   a black songbird

blackboard   a smooth board, once black, now colored, for writing on with chalk

blackcurrant   a small black berry

blacksmith   a man who makes and mends iron things. He also puts metal shoes on horses.

blade   one leaf of grass or wheat. The same word also means the cutting part of a knife.

blame   to find fault with

blank   without any writing or marks, empty

blanket   a bedcover made out of wool or other material

blast   an explosion: a strong sudden gust of air

blaze   a brightly burning fire

bleach   to take the color out of something

bleak   cold and windy: without cheer

bleat   the crying sound made by a lamb, sheep or goat

bleed   to lose blood

blend   to mix together

bless   to make holy; to ask God to show favor to someone or something

blind   not able to see

blink   to open and shut your eyes very quickly

blister   a swelling on the skin, like a small bubble, often filled with water or blood

blizzard   a very windy snow storm

block   a big piece of something, like wood, metal or stone. The same word also means to be in the way of something.

blood   the red liquid that circulates round your body

bloom   to come into flower

blossom   another name for flower, especially the flowers on fruit trees and shrubs

blot   a spot or mark, usually of ink.

blouse a loose garment covering the upper part of the body. It is worn by girls and women.

blow to push air out of your mouth. The same word also means a hard knock.

blue a color. When the sun shines the sky is blue.

bluebell a wild flower with blue blossoms shaped like bells

blunt the opposite of sharp, having a dull edge or point

blur to make something look dim or not clear

blush to go pink in the face because you are shy, ashamed or upset by something

boar a male pig

board a long flat piece of wood

boarder someone who pays to eat and sleep in a person's house

boarding school a school where children live during the school year

boast to talk a lot about how good you are at things, to praise yourself or things which belong to you

boat a small ship

bob to move up and down

bobbin   a spool for holding thread or yarn

bodice   the part of a dress from the neck to the waist. It is usually close-fitting.

body   the whole of a person or animal

bodyguard   a person who guards and protects someone

bog   wet, marshy ground

boil   to make water so hot that it bubbles and makes steam. The same word also means a sore swelling on your body.

boiler   a container for boiling water, often for making steam

bold   brave; without fear

bolt   a metal fastening for doors and gates. The same word also means to run away.

bomb   a metal case that can be exploded

bomber   an airplane which carries bombs

bond   anything which binds or fastens something together

bone   one of the hard white parts which are joined together to make the skeletons of our bodies

bonfire   a fire out of doors, usually in a garden

bonnet   a kind of hat that ties under the chin

book   pages of print bound together in a cover

bookcase   a set of shelves for books

boom   a long deep noise, like the sound the word
       boom makes when you say it

boomerang   a curved wooden weapon
       that turns in the air and comes back
       to the person who throws it

boot   a shoe that covers part of the leg as well as
       the foot

bootee   a soft woolen boot for babies

border   the outside edge of something

bore   to make a deep hole in something by twisting
       a tool round and round. The same word
       also means to make someone tired by dull talk.

born   starting to live

borrow   to take something which you intend to give
       back

bosom   another word for breast. The same word
       also means close, like a bosom friend.

boss   a chief or leader

botany   the study of plants

bother   to annoy or worry. The same word also
       means fuss or trouble.

bottle   a container, usually made of glass. It has a
       narrow neck and is used to hold liquids.

bottom   the lowest part of anything

bough (*rhymes with now*)   the branch of a tree

boulder   a very large rock or stone

bounce   to spring up again after hitting the ground

bound   to leap forward. The same word also means fastened or tied.

bouquet (*say bookay*)   a bunch of flowers

bow (*rhymes with so*)   a kind of knot used to tie ribbon or string. The same word also means a curved strip of wood with a string, used for shooting arrows.

bow (*rhymes with now*)   a way of showing respect. You bend forward and lower your head.

bowl   a deep round dish for holding liquids or food

box   a stiff-sided container

boxer   a man who fights with his fists, usually in padded gloves

boy   a male child who will grow up to be a man

bracelet   a pretty chain or ring you wear on your arm

bracket   a piece of metal or wood that holds a shelf up

brag   another word for boast

braid   to weave strips of hair or material in and out to make a plait

brain   the part inside your head that sends and receives messages and thoughts and controls what your body does

brake   the part of a vehicle which stops the wheels from going round

bramble   a blackberry bush

bran   the skin of grains, which is separated from the flour

branch   the arm of a tree that grows out of its trunk

brand   a mark on something to show whose it is or who made it

brass   a yellowish metal made by melting copper and zinc together

brave   not running away from danger, even when you are afraid

brawn   strength; powerful muscle

bray   the cry of a donkey

bread   a food made mostly from flour, and baked into a loaf

breadth   how wide or broad something is

break   to pull apart; to damage or spoil something

breakfast   the first meal of the day

breast   the top front part of the body

breath   the air that is taken in and forced out by the lungs

breathe   to take air into the body and force it out again

breed   to produce young ones

breeze   a gentle wind

brewery   a place where beer is made

brick   a block of baked clay used in building

bride   a woman on her wedding day

bridesmaid   an unmarried woman who attends the bride on her wedding day

bridge   something built over a road or river so that you can get across to the other side

brief   short; not long

brigade   a group of men in uniform who work together, like a brigade of soldiers or a brigade of firemen

bright   shining; giving out light

brilliant   very bright; dazzling. The same word also means very clever.

brim   the upper edge of something, like the brim of a cup. The same word also means the part of a hat that sticks out all round.

bring   to carry something with you when you come

brisk   quick; lively

bristle   a short stiff hair

brittle   easily broken

broad   wide; the opposite of narrow

broadcast   to send out radio or television programs of news, music and entertainment

bronchitis   an illness in the throat and chest that makes you cough a lot

bronze a reddish-brown metal made by melting copper and tin together

brooch (*say broach*) an ornament which can be pinned to clothing

brood to sit quietly and think about something rather anxiously. The same word also means young birds all hatched in one nest at the same time.

brook a small stream

broom a brush with a long handle, for cleaning floors

broth a kind of thin soup

brother a son of the same parents

brow the forehead

brown a color. Chocolate is brown.

brownie a junior member of the Girl Scouts. The same word also means a kind of goblin who is supposed to help with housework.

bruise a dark-colored mark where the skin has been hit but not broken

brush a bunch of hairs on a handle, used for cleaning or painting or doing your hair

bubble a ball of liquid containing gas or air

bucket a container with a handle for holding or carrying water

buckle a fastening on a belt or strap

bud a flower or leaf not fully open

budge   to move a little

buffalo   a wild ox

bug   a tiny insect

build   to make or construct

builder   a man who puts up buildings

building   anything with a roof and walls

bulb   a small glass lamp which gives out electric light. The same word also means the rounded root from which some flowers grow.

bulge   to swell out

bulk   a large amount

bull   the male of cattle. Male elephants are also called bulls.

bulldog   a heavily-built dog with a large head and powerful shoulders

bulldozer   a powerful tractor used for shifting large loads of earth, sand or rubbish

bullet   a small piece of metal which is shot from a gun

bullfrog   a large frog with a deep voice

bullock   a young bull

bully   someone who picks on others weaker or smaller than himself

bulrush a kind of tall reed that grows in or near water

bumblebee a large fluffy bee which makes a loud buzzing noise

bump a swelling, or a raised part of anything. The same word also means to knock into something.

bumper a piece of curved metal on the front and back of cars to protect them if they bump into something

bun a small soft round cake

bunch a group of things tied or growing together, like a bunch of flowers

bundle a number of articles bound together, like a bundle of clothes

bungalow a house without an upstairs

bunk a shelf-like bed attached to a wall

buoy (*say boy*) something floating on the water but anchored to the sea bed. It marks the places where there is danger, or where small boats can be tied up.

burden a load that is very heavy to carry

bureau a chest of drawers. The same word also means a special department of the government.

burglar someone who breaks into buildings at night and steals things

burial   the burying of something, like a dead body, in the ground

burn   to be on fire, or to set something on fire

burrow   a hole in the ground which has been dug by wild animals to live in. Rabbits and foxes live in burrows.

burst   to give way suddenly; to rush forward

bury   to put something somewhere deep, usually under the ground

bus   a large vehicle which carries a large number of people

bush   a shrub, like a small tree with lots of branches growing close to the ground

business (*say bizness*)   occupation, work

bust   a sculpture of someone's head, shoulders and chest. Sometimes the word means the breast.

bustle   to rush about busily

busy   having something to do all the time; working hard

butcher   a man who cuts up meat and sells it

butter   a kind of soft yellow fat made from cream

buttercup   a bright yellow wildflower

butterfly   an insect with large colored wings

butterscotch   a sweet made from sugar and butter

buttocks   the two rounded parts which you sit on, at the back of your body below the waist

button   a round fastening on clothes; any small knob

buttonhole   a narrow hole for a button to fit into

buy   to give money in exchange for something

buzz   the humming sound a bee makes

cab   the place in an engine or truck where the driver sits. The same word also means a taxi.

cabbage   a vegetable with green or purple leaves growing tightly together in a round ball

cabin   a small house or hut made of logs or other rough materials. The same word also means a room for passengers on a ship or airplane.

cabinet   a kind of cupboard with glass doors where you keep ornaments or collections of things

cable   a very strong thick rope, sometimes made of pieces of wire twisted together

cackle   the loud excited noise made by hens

cactus   a plant with thick leaves and stems, often covered with prickles, which grows in hot dry countries. You can also grow small ones as house plants.

caddy   a small airtight box to keep tea in

cadet   a boy or young man who is learning to be an officer in the army or navy or air force

café (*say caffay*)   a place where you can buy a meal or a snack; a small restaurant

cafeteria   an eating-place where you get your own food from a counter

cage   a box or room with bars, where birds or animals are kept

cake   a sweet food made of flour, fat, eggs and sugar and baked in an oven. The same word also means a small flat lump of something, like a cake of soap.

calamity   something awful that happens, like an earthquake or an airplane crash in which many people are killed or hurt

calendar   a list of all the days and dates in each week and each month of a year

calf   a young cow or bull. The same word also means the thick part of the back of your leg below the knee.

call   to shout or cry out. The same word also means to stop at someone's house for a short time.

calm   quiet; still. The same word also means not getting upset or excited when something unusual happens.

camel   a big animal with a long neck and one or two humps on its back. It carries people or things from place to place in some hot countries.

camera   a kind of box for taking photographs

camouflage   to disguise something so that it is hidden from the enemy

camp   to live outdoors in a tent. The same word also means the place where the tents are set up.

can   a small airtight metal container for food or liquids. The same word also means to be able to do something.

canal   a very big ditch, dug across land and filled with water so that ships and boats can move along it

canary   a small yellow bird kept as a pet because of its sweet song

candle   a rounded stick of wax with a wick through the middle. It burns and gives light.

candy   a sweet food made of sugar or syrup, and other things such as chocolate and nuts

cane   the hard stem of a plant or small palm tree. The same word also means a light walking stick.

cannon   a big heavy gun, sometimes on wheels

canoe   a narrow light boat. You use a paddle to make it move through the water.

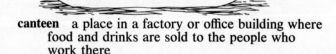

canteen   a place in a factory or office building where food and drinks are sold to the people who work there

canvas   tough strong cloth used for tents and sails and for painting pictures on

cap   a small soft hat, usually with a peak

capacity   the greatest amount a container will hold

cape   a piece of clothing without sleeves that goes over the back and shoulders and fastens round the neck. The same word also means a point of land sticking out into the sea.

caper to leap or jump about happily

capital a large letter of the alphabet, like A, B, C. The same word also means the chief city in a country.

capsule a tiny container for medicine, which melts after you have swallowed it. The same word also means the closed cabin of a spacecraft.

captain a person who is in charge of a group of people, like soldiers, sailors or a football team

captive someone who has been captured and held prisoner

capture to catch someone and hold him by force

car an automobile

caramel a kind of sweet, like toffee, made with sugar and butter cooked together until the mixture is sticky and brown

caravan a small house on wheels, pulled by a car or a horse. The same word also means a group of people traveling together for safety, especially in the desert.

carburetor part of a car engine that mixes air and gas

card stiff paper. Sometimes it is cut into pieces with pictures and greetings for special days like birthdays and Christmas. Cards are also used in playing games.

cardboard very thick stiff paper

cardigan a knitted woolen jacket

care a worry or trouble. The same word also means to look after someone who needs help.

careful giving special attention to what you are doing

careless not taking trouble or thinking about what you are doing

caretaker a person who looks after a building or part of a building

cargo a ship's load

carnation a pink, red, yellow or white flower with a spicy smell

carol a song of joy or praise, most often heard at Christmas time

carpenter a man who makes things out of wood such as tables, chairs and cupboards

carpet a thick soft woven covering for the floor, sometimes made of wool

carriage a vehicle for carrying passengers from place to place

carrot a long pointed orange vegetable that grows under the ground

carry to take something from one place to another

cart an open wagon with only two wheels, usually pulled by a horse

cartoon a short funny film or drawing in a newspaper

cartridge a case for holding the gunpowder and bullet to be shot from a gun

carve   to shape a piece of wood or to cut patterns on it with a knife. The same word also means to cut meat into slices.

case   a kind of box to keep or carry things in

cash   coins and banknotes

cashier   someone who looks after the money in a bank, a shop or an office

cast   to throw something with force. The same word also means to shape something by pouring hot metal or liquid plaster into a mold.

castaway   a person who has been shipwrecked

castle   an old building with thick stone walls to resist enemy attacks

cat   a furry animal, usually kept as a pet

catalogue   a list of things in a special order, like a list of books in a library

catch   to get hold of something

caterpillar   a grub that turns into a moth or butterfly

cathedral   a very large and important church

catkins   small fluffy flowers without petals. They grow on willow and hazel trees.

cattle   cows, bulls and oxen

cauliflower a cabbage-like vegetable with a large white part in the middle that is good to eat

cause to make something happen

caution carefulness; watchfulness

cavalry soldiers on horseback

cave a big hole in rocks or in the side of a hill

cavern a large cave

caw the loud hoarse cry of a crow

cease to stop

ceiling the top of a room

celandine a yellow wildflower

celebration a party on a special day like a birthday or a national holiday

celery a vegetable with long white stalks and pale green leaves

cell a room where prisoners are kept. The same word also means the small bare room a monk lives in.

cellar an underground room where coal and wine and other things are kept

cement a grayish powdered clay mixture that hardens when it is mixed with sand and water. It is used to stick bricks and other building materials together.

cemetery a place where people who have died are buried

center the middle part of anything

centigrade divided into a hundred degrees. On a centigrade thermometer freezing point is shown as zero and boiling point at 100.

centimeter a hundredth part of a meter

century a hundred years

cereal any kind of grain used as food

ceremony an important and special happening, like a wedding or a coronation

certain sure; without any doubt

certificate something written or printed which proves that something is true; written proof that you have passed an examination

chain metal rings joined together

chair a single seat with a back to lean against

chalet (*say shalay*) a small wooden house, usually with overhanging eaves

chalk a soft white stone which can be made into sticks for writing on the blackboard. Sometimes chalk is colored.

challenge to invite someone to try to beat you at something, such as running, swimming or wrestling

champion someone who is better at a sport than anyone else. The same word also means to stick up for someone or defend him.

chance something that happens without being planned. The same word also means an opportunity.

change to make something different from what it was before

channel a deep narrow strip of sea-water between two pieces of land. The same word also means a kind of path through the air used for television programs.

chapel a small church or a separate part of a large church

chapter a section of a book divided off by numbers—chapter 1, chapter 2

character what a person is like. Someone's character may be good or bad, honest or dishonest, nice or nasty.

charade (*say sharade*) a game in which you act out parts of a word and then the whole word and people have to guess what it is

charcoal a hard blackened piece of burnt wood. You can draw pictures with it.

charge the cost of something. The same word also means to rush at something. To be in charge is to be in control.

chariot an open two-wheeled carriage drawn by horses. In olden days chariots were used in wars and in races.

charity   a feeling of kindness and affection towards other people: a gift of money, food or shelter to people in need

charm   to make others think you are nice and pleasant to know. The same word also means something that has magic powers or can bring good luck.

chart   a map, usually of the sea

chase   to run after

chassis (*say shassee*)   the framework which forms the base of a car

chat   to talk with someone in a friendly way

chatter   to talk a lot about unimportant things

chatterbox   someone who is always talking

chauffeur (*say shofer*)   a man who is paid to drive someone else's car

cheap   not costing much money

cheat   to do something that is not honest or right, like copying someone else's answers during a test

check   to go back over something to make sure it is correct. The same word also means a special piece of paper you write on to ask your bank to pay some of your money to someone.

cheek   the soft side of your face below your eyes and either side of your nose

cheer   to shout at someone to do his best or to show you are pleased. The same word also means joy, happiness.

cheerful   happy; joyful

cheese   a food made from milk

chemistry   the study of what things are made of

cherry   a sweet round red or yellow fruit with a stone in it

cherub   a winged creature with a child's face

chess   a game for two people, using pieces called chessmen on a board marked with black and white squares

chest   a large strong box with a lid. The same word also means the front part of your body between your neck and your waist.

chestnut   a nut. One kind is good to eat when it is roasted, but not the other kind which is called a horse chestnut.

chew   to crush or grind with your teeth

chewing gum   a kind of candy that you keep chewing but do not swallow

chick   a baby bird

chicken   a young hen or cock

chicken-pox   an illness. You have a high temperature and lots of spots all over you.

chief   a leader or ruler. We also use the word to mean that something is the most important, like the chief city in a country.

chilblain   a painful itchy swelling on your hands or feet in cold weather

child   a boy or girl who is older than a baby, but who is not yet grown up

children   boys and girls

chilly   feeling cold

chime   a musical sound made by a set of bells, usually in a clock

chimney   an opening from the fireplace to the roof to let the smoke out

chimpanzee   a very clever ape, smaller than a gorilla

chin   the part of your face under your mouth

china   cups and plates made from a kind of clay

chink   a narrow crack or slit. The same word also means a clinking sound, as when you rattle coins together.

chip   to knock a small piece off something like a cup or vase. The same word also means a small piece of fried potato.

chipmunk   a small wild animal, like a squirrel with stripes

chirp   a short shrill sound made by some birds and insects

chisel   a tool with a cutting edge at the end, used for cutting stone or wood

chocolate   a sweet brown food or drink made from cocoa

choir (*say kwire*)   a group of people trained to sing together

choke   to find it hard to breathe because there is something in your throat or because there is smoke in your lungs

choose   to take one thing rather than another

chop   to cut something with hard blows. The same word also means a small piece of meat on a bone.

chopper   something you use to chop with, like an ax

chopsticks   two thin pieces of wood or ivory used for eating food by people living in some far-eastern countries

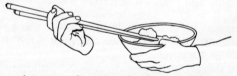

chorus   the part of a song that comes after each verse, when everyone joins in the singing. The same word means the people on a stage who dance and sing together.

christen   to give a baby its first or Christian name, usually in a church

Christian   a follower of Jesus Christ

Christmas   the birthday of Jesus Christ

chrome   a silvery-looking metal

chrysanthemum an autumn flower with lots of brightly colored curving petals

chuck to throw

chuckle to laugh quietly

chum a close friend

church a building where people go to worship God

churn a machine for making butter: a large milk can

cigar tobacco leaves rolled tightly together, for smoking

cigarette finely cut pieces of tobacco rolled in thin paper, for smoking

cinders coal or wood that has been burned but not burned away to ashes

circle a completely round ring

circulate to move around and come back to the beginning. The blood in our veins circulates through every part of our bodies.

circus a traveling show with acrobats and animals and clowns who do all sorts of tricks

city a very large town

civil to do with people or the government, like the civil service, but not the armed forces. The same word means polite.

claim to demand something because you believe you should have it

clang a loud deep echoing noise, usually made by big bells

clank a deep ringing sound such as the noise made by rattling heavy chains

clap to slap the palms of your hands together

clash a loud noise when things are banged together

clasp to hold tightly. The same word also means a fastening for a brooch or other jewelry.

class a number of children or older people learning something together

classroom a room in school where children learn things

clatter a rattling noise, as when you are washing dishes and cutlery

claw one of the sharp curved nails on the foot of an animal or bird

clay soft sticky earth that can be baked to make bricks or pottery

clean without dirt or dust

cleaner someone or something that cleans things

cleanse to make clean

clear bright, or with nothing in the way, so that you can see things easily

clench to close your teeth or fists tightly together

clerk someone who does office work, such as answering letters and keeping accounts

clever quick to learn; able to do things very well

click a short snapping sound

cliff a high steep rock

climate the kind of weather a country usually has.
Africa and India have hot climates.

climb to move upwards using your feet and
sometimes your hands to hold on

cling to hold on to something tightly

clinic a place where people go to see doctors or
nurses

clink a small ringing sound, as when you gently
touch coins or glasses together

clip to cut or trim something with scissors. The
same word also means a small metal fastening
for holding letters or papers together.

clipper a large fast ship with many sails

cloak a loose garment without sleeves, usually
longer than a cape

cloakroom a place where you can leave hats and
coats

clock a machine that tells you what the time is

clockwise the direction in which clock hands move

clockwork machinery like that which is inside a
clock

clog to block up something like a drainpipe. The
same word also means a wooden shoe.

close to shut. The same word also means very near.

cloth a woven material that clothes and coverings are made of

clothes all the things you wear, except jewelry

clothing another word for clothes

cloud millions of tiny drops of water floating close together in the sky. Clouds may look white or gray.

clout a blow. The same word also means a piece of cloth.

clover a wild plant with leaves in three rounded parts and small tight pink or white heads

clown a man in a circus. He has a funny painted face and makes us laugh.

club a group of people who meet to do things together, like playing tennis or golf. The same word also means a heavy stick.

cluck the soft short sound a hen makes to her chicks

clue something that helps you to find the answer to a puzzle or mystery

clump a number of plants or trees growing close together

clumsy not graceful; not good at handling things

cluster a bunch; a group

clutch to grab something and hold on to it tightly. The same word also means a part of machinery used for starting and stopping an engine.

coach a large carriage pulled by horses, with an

outside seat in front for the driver. The same word also means a large motor vehicle for long journeys.

coal   a hard black mineral used for fuel

coalman   a man who delivers coal

coarse   rough

coast   the border of land next to the sea. The same word also means to go downhill in a car without using the engine, or on a bicycle without pedalling.

coat   an outer garment with sleeves

cobbler   someone who makes or mends boots and shoes

cobweb   a very thin net made by a spider to trap insects

cock   a male bird: a rooster

cockerel   a young cock

cocoa   a brown powder made from cocoa beans. It is used to make hot drinks and chocolate.

coconut   a very large nut with milky liquid inside

cod   a large sea fish caught for food

code   secret words or signals used to send messages

coffee   a hot drink made from ground-up roasted coffee beans

coffin a large wooden or metal box that a dead body is put into

coil to wind in rings

coin a piece of money made of metal

coke fuel made from coal when the gas has been baked out of it

cold the opposite of hot. A fire is hot and ice is cold. The same word also means an illness which affects the nose and throat.

collapse to fall to pieces or to fall down

collar the part of a garment round the neck

collect to bring together or gather together

collection the things you collect, such as a collection of stamps, seashells or old coins

college a place where you can go on studying after you have left secondary school

collide to bump or run into something

collie a large longhaired sheepdog

colliery a coal mine

color Red, yellow, blue and green are colors.

colt a young horse

column a pillar. The same word also means a line of soldiers and a list of numbers.

comb a short piece of plastic or metal with teeth in it, used to tidy your hair

combine to mix or join together

combine-harvester   a farm machine that does two jobs. It harvests the grain and then threshes it.

come   to move near

comedian   an actor who makes people laugh

comedy   a funny play or film

comfortable   to be feeling at ease, without pain or worry

comic   a picture paper for children

command   to tell someone he must do something

commence   to begin

commit   to do something, usually something wrong like a crime

committee   a small number of people who meet together to arrange things

common   ordinary; usual. The same word also means an open piece of ground that doesn't belong to one person.

commotion   noise and fuss

companion   someone who goes somewhere with you; a friend

company   a group of people working together in a business. The same word also means a group of people who are guests at a party.

compare   to say how things are alike or different; to show whether one thing is better or worse than another

compass   an instrument for showing north, south, east and west

compasses   a tool for drawing a circle

compel   to force someone to do something

compete   to be in a test or race to see who is best

competition   a test of how much people know or how good they are at something. The winner usually gets a prize.

complain   to tell about something that is upsetting you, or that you think is wrong

complete   whole, with nothing missing

complicated   not easy or simple; difficult to understand

compliment   something nice said about someone to please him

composition   things put together to make a whole thing. A number of notes make a musical composition, and words written down make a written composition.

comprehension   the ability to understand

compress   to press together

conceal   to hide; to keep secret

conceited   thinking too highly of yourself

concentrate   to bring together in one place: to think hard about one thing

concern   to do with; to interest or trouble yourself with

concert   a musical entertainment

conclude   to end or finish something

concrete a mixture of cement, gravel and water that dries as hard as stone

condense to make something smaller or shorter by taking part of it away. Condensed milk has some of the liquid taken out of it to make it thicker and smaller in quantity.

condition how something or someone is

conduct to guide; to lead; to be in charge. The same word also means behavior.

conductor someone who collects bus or train tickets. The same word also means a man who stands in front of an orchestra and beats time.

cone something round at the bottom and pointed at the top, like an ice cream cone or a clown's hat. The same word also means the fruits of pine or fir trees, which are cone-shaped.

confess to say that you have done wrong; to own up to something

confetti tiny bits of colored paper thrown at a wedding for good luck

conflict a fight or struggle

confuse to mix up; to mistake one thing for another

congratulate to tell a person you are glad about something good that has happened to him

congregation people gathered together in a church

conjuror someone who can do magic tricks

connect to join or fasten together

conquer to win; to overcome

conscious knowing what is going on; able to hear and understand what is happening around you

consent to agree

conservatory a heated greenhouse where plants can be grown

consider to think carefully about something

considerable rather large; much

considerate kind to others; thoughtful about how other people feel

consonants the sounds of a language other than vowels. They are written by all the letters of the alphabet except *a e i o u.*

construct to build or make

contain to hold something inside. A bottle contains milk.

container something that holds things inside, such as a box or bottle

contented happy; pleased with what you have

contents what is contained in something

continual keeping on; frequent

continue to go on doing something, or to begin doing something again

continuous keeping on without stopping

contract to become smaller. The same word also means an agreement.

contradict to disagree entirely; to say that something someone has said is not true

control to guide or curb something, such as a vehicle or a machine. The same word also means to be in command of other people.

convenient easy to use or reach

convent a building for nuns to live in

conversation talk between two or more people

convict someone who has been sent to prison

convince to persuade someone that you are right

cook to heat food and make it ready for eating

cookery the art or practice of cooking

cool not quite cold

copper a reddish-brown metal

copy to make or do something exactly the same as something else

coral a hard, stony pink or white material made from millions of piled-up skeletons of tiny sea animals, sometimes used to make jewelry

corduroy cotton cloth with ridges in it

core the middle part of something, like the part where the seeds are in an apple or pear

corgi a small dog with short legs

cork a stopper put in the top of a bottle to keep the liquid from spilling out

corn the seeds of grain plants, like wheat, barley and oats. The same word also means a hard lump of skin on your toe, that hurts when your shoe is too tight.

corner where two walls or roads meet

cornet a musical instrument like a trumpet. The same word also means an ice cream in a kind of biscuit shaped like a cone.

cornflakes a breakfast cereal eaten cold with milk and sugar

cornflower a bright blue summer flower

coronation the crowning of a king or queen

corporation a group of people who run the business of a company or town

correct right; true; with no mistakes

corridor a long narrow passage with rooms leading off it

cost what you have to pay for something

costly expensive; not cheap

costume style of clothing worn at different times in history. The same word also means clothes worn by actors on the stage.

cosy comfortable: snug and warm

cot a bed for a small child

cottage a small house in the country

cotton thread or yarn made from the cotton plant. The same word also means the cloth woven from cotton.

cottonwool   the fluffy part of the cotton plant

couch   a long soft seat where more than one person can sit

cough   the loud noise you make when you choke or when you have a sore throat or bronchitis

council   a group of people who meet to talk and decide about problems to do with controlling a town or city

count   to name numbers in their proper order. The same word also means a nobleman.

countdown   the counting backwards of seconds of time before a rocket is fired

counter   a kind of long table in a shop or café

counter-clockwise   the opposite direction to the way clock hands move

country   the land outside a town. Another country means another part of the world.

county   a part or section of a country

couple   two of anything; a pair

coupon   a printed piece of paper which can be exchanged for something else

courage   without fear even when there is danger; bravery

course   the direction in which anything goes. The same word also means a number of lessons on one special subject.

court   the place where a king or a judge works

courtyard   an enclosed space near or within a building

cousin   the child of your aunt or uncle

cover   to put one thing over another so as to hide it

cow   the female of cattle

coward   someone who is not brave

cowboy   a man on a ranch
who looks after cattle

cowshed   a farm building where cattle are kept

cowslip   the marsh marigold

crab   a water animal with a hard shell and
big claws

crack   a split or long thin opening in something. The
same word also means a sharp, sudden noise.

cracker   a thin crisp biscuit

crackle   a crisp sound, like the sound made by the
word when you say it. Dry twigs crackle on a
fire.

cradle   a baby's bed with rockers instead of legs

craftsman   someone who is good at making things
with his hands

crafty   artful; cunning

crane   a machine for lifting heavy things. The same
word also means a long-legged bird.

crash   a loud smashing noise

crate   a container for packing vegetables, eggs, fruit
and bottles. It is made of thin pieces of wood
fastened together.

crawl   to move forward on your hands and knees. The same word means a stroke used in swimming.

crayon   a soft kind of pencil that you use to color a picture

crazy   silly; mad

cream   the rich fatty part of milk

creamery   a place where butter and cheese are made or sold

crease   a mark made by folding or doubling something like paper or cloth

create   to make or bring into being

creator   maker or producer

creature   a living thing, such as a bird, insect or other animal

creek   a small stream or part of a river

creep   to move slowly and quietly, sometimes on your hands and knees

crêpe (*say crayp*)   thin wrinkly cloth

crescent   anything shaped like the new moon

cress   a plant used in salads

crew   people who work on a ship or airplane

crib   a small bed with bars to keep a young child from falling out

cricket   an insect something like a grasshopper, which makes a chirping sound

crime something wrong that can be punished by law

crimson a deep red color with some blue in it

crinkle to wrinkle something by squeezing it tightly

cripple a person who is lame or whose arms or legs have been damaged in some way

crisp hard and dry; easily broken, like a potato chip or a piece of toast

crisscross straight lines crossing over each other

croak a deep, hoarse noise, like the sound a frog makes

crock a pot or a jar

crocodile a dangerous scaly reptile which lives in or near water in hot countries

crocus a small garden plant, with bright purple, yellow or white flowers

crook someone who is not honest. The same word also means a long hooked stick or staff carried by shepherds.

crooked not straight

crop grain, fruit or vegetables grown on the land for food. The same word also means a short whip used in horseback riding.

cross anything shaped like × or +. The same word also means rather angry.

crow a large black bird, with a harsh croaking voice. The same word also means the sound a cock makes.

crowd a lot of people all together in one place

crown   the gold head dress worn by a king or queen

cruel   very unkind

cruise   a sea voyage for pleasure

crumb   a very small piece of bread, cake or biscuit

crumble   to break into little pieces

crumple   to crush something into wrinkles

crunch   to make a loud noise when you are chewing something hard and crisp like an apple or toast

crush   to press together or squash something

crust   the hard outer covering of something like a loaf of bread or a pie

crutch   a special stick with a padded top piece that fits under the armpit. Lame people use crutches to help them to walk.

cry   to weep tears. The same word also means to make a loud sound of joy or sorrow.

crystal   a hard mineral that is transparent

cub   the name given to some young animals such as bears and foxes

cube   a shape having six sides of equal measurement, like a cube of sugar

cuckoo   a bird that lays its eggs in other birds' nests. It makes a noise that sounds like its name, cuckoo.

cucumber   a long green watery vegetable used in salads

cuddle   to hug with affection

cue   a stick used in the game of billiards

cuff   the end of a sleeve at the wrist. The same word also means a blow with the palm of your hand.

cunning   clever in a rather unpleasant way; crafty

cup   a small bowl-shaped container with a handle, used for drinking

cupboard   a set of shelves with doors

curb   to stop or hold something back. The same word also means the edge of a pavement.

curds   the thick part of milk, when it is separated to make cheese. The thin watery part is called whey.

cure   to help someone who is ill to get well again; to heal

curious   wanting to know or find out. The same word also means odd or strange.

curl   to twist hair into curves or rings

curlers   rollers or pins which girls and women put into their hair to make it curly

curly   not straight; going around in curves

currant   a small dried grape: a red, black or white sour-tasting berry that grows on bushes

current   a flow or stream of air, water or electricity. The same word also means at present, happening now.

curtain   a piece of cloth hanging down to cover a window or a stage in a theater

curtsy   a bow girls and women make by bending their knees

curve   a line shaped like part of a circle

cushion   a soft pillow covered with pretty material. It is used to rest against on a chair or settee.

custard   milk, eggs and sugar cooked together to make a pudding or sauce

custom   what is usually done; habit

customer   someone who wants to buy something, usually in a shop

cut   to make pieces of something smaller by using scissors or a knife

cutlery   what you eat food with — knives, forks and spoons

cycle   another word for bicycle

cyclone   a very bad storm in which a strong wind goes round and round in a circle

cylinder   a hollow rounded piece of metal often used in machinery

cymbals   two metal musical instruments, shaped like plates

dab   to touch something lightly

daffodil   a yellow spring flower shaped rather like a trumpet

daft   foolish or silly

dagger   a short sword

dahlia   a garden plant with brightly colored flowers

daily   every day

dainty   pretty; delicate

dairy   a place where milk, butter and cheese are kept

daisy   a small field flower with white or pink petals around a yellow center

dale   low ground between hills; a small valley

dam   a special kind of wall which checks a flow of water

damage   harm or injury

damp   slightly wet

dance   to move in time to music

dandelion   a wild plant with bright yellow flowers

danger   risk; the opposite of safety

dangerous   not safe

dare   to have the courage to do something

daring   full of courage; plucky

dark   without light. When the sun goes down, the sky grows dark.

darling   someone dearly loved. We may call a person or animal we love, darling.

darn to mend a hole by sewing it over with wool or cotton

dart a kind of small arrow thrown by hand

dartboard the target at which you aim in the game of darts

dash to rush suddenly. The same word also means a short straight line in writing, like this —.

date a time when something happens; a certain hour, day, month or year. The same word also means a sweet sticky fruit with a pit.

daughter a female child of a father and a mother

dawdle to waste time

dawn the first light of day

day the time between sunrise and sunset

dazed being confused or bewildered

dazzle to blind someone for a short time by suddenly shining a strong bright light into his eyes

dead without life

deaf not able to hear

deal an amount. The same word also means to do business with.

dear much loved, precious. The same word also means highly priced.

death the end of life

debt what someone owes to someone else

decay to become rotten or to fall into ruins

deceive to make someone believe something that is not true; to cheat

decent proper; acceptable to most people

decide to make up your mind; to settle something

decimal numbered by tens

deck the flooring on a boat or ship

declare to say something clearly; to make something known

decorate to make something look pretty. We decorate a Christmas tree.

deed an act; something done

deep a long way down

deer a wild animal with four long legs. The male has large branched horns.

defeat to beat someone at a game; to conquer

defend to try to keep yourself from being beaten; to guard someone or something against attack

definite certain; without doubt

defy to refuse to obey

degree a unit of measurement. Temperature is measured in degrees centigrade or degrees fahrenheit.

delay   to put off to a later time

deliberate   not by accident; done on purpose

delicate   easily broken or damaged; fragile

delicatessen   a shop that sells food ready to eat, such as cooked meats or special cheeses and salads

delicious   very good to taste and eat

delight   great pleasure or joy

deliver   to hand something over to someone else. The same word also means to rescue or set free.

dell   a little valley in a wood or forest

demand   to ask for something in a commanding way, without saying please

demon   an evil spirit or devil

den   a cave or shelter where some kinds of wild animals live

dense   closely-packed; thick; difficult to make your way through, like a dense forest

dent   a bent place in something, usually caused by a blow

dentist   someone who takes care of your teeth

deny   to say that something someone says is not true

depart   to go away or leave a place

department   a part or section of a shop, office or factory

depend to count on someone; to rely

deposit to put something down and leave it. The same word also means a small amount of money left in part payment for something.

depot (*say deepo*) a storehouse; a railroad station

depth how deep something is

descend to go down

describe to say what something or someone is like

desert land on which very little can grow because there is no water. Deserts are often made of sand.

deserve to earn something, like deserving a reward for working hard

design to draw a pattern; to make a plan or drawing

desire to want something very much. The same word also means a wish or request.

desk a table used for reading or writing

despair to give up hope

despise to dislike something or someone very much because you think they are no good and worthless

dessert the fruit or pudding served after the main part of a meal

destroy to kill or ruin completely

destroyer a warship that guards a fleet of ships against attack

detail a small part

determine to settle or decide; to make up your mind to do something

detest to hate very much

develop to grow gradually, as a puppy develops into a dog, or a bud develops into a flower

devil an evil spirit. The word is often used to describe a wicked or cruel person.

dew drops of moisture which cover the ground in the very early morning

diagonal a line drawn from one corner of something to the opposite corner

diagram a plan or drawing to show what a thing is, or how it works

dial the flat round part of something with numbers on it, like a clock, a watch or a telephone

dialect a special way of speaking a language in one part of a country

diameter a straight line drawn from one side of a circle to the other, passing through the center

diamond a very hard colorless precious stone which sparkles

diary a book in which you write down what you do from day to day

dice a pair of small cubes with different numbers of spots on each side. They are used in games.

---

dictionary   a book which tells you the meanings of words and how to spell them

die   to stop living or to come to an end. The same word also means one of a pair of dice.

diesel engine   an engine that burns a special kind of oil

differ   to be unlike; to disagree

difference   what makes something not like something else

different   not the same

difficult   hard to do or to understand

dig   to make a hole in the ground

dignified   acting in a serious manner

dim   not bright

dimple   a little hollow, usually in your cheek or chin

din   loud noise, usually going on for a long time

dine   to eat dinner

dingy   dull and dirty looking

dinner   the main meal of the day

dinosaur   a very large reptile that lived millions and millions of years ago

dip   to go in and out of something quickly. You dip your spoon into a bowl of soup.

dire dreadful; terrible

direct straight; the quickest or shortest way. The same word also means to show someone the way.

direction the way something goes, such as a road going north, south, east or west

dirt mud, soil, or earth

dirty not clean; in need of washing

disagree to have a different opinion about something

disappear to go away very quickly; to vanish

disappoint to find that things are not as you had hoped they would be. When you do not win a game you may be disappointed.

disaster a calamity; a great misfortune

disc anything which is round and flat, such as a record

disciple a follower or pupil

discourage to make someone feel that what he is doing is not worth while so that he will stop trying

discover to find out; to see something for the first time

discovery something which has been found out

discuss to talk about

discussion an argument or talk with other people

disease illness; sickness

disgrace   shame

disguise   to change your appearance by wearing different clothes, a wig or a false moustache, so that people do not recognize you

disgust   a feeling of dislike so strong that it makes you feel sick

dish   a plate for food

dishonest   the opposite of honest

dislike   the opposite of like

dismay   fear; a feeling of being upset and sad

dismiss   to send someone away or tell him they can leave

distance   the length of space between two places

distant   far away. A far-off place is distant.

distemper   an illness which young dogs get

distinct   separate; clearly seen or heard

distress   a feeling of great pain, sorrow or worry

district   a part of a town or county

disturb   to interrupt or cause trouble

disturbance   a noisy interruption, as when people upset a meeting by shouting out

ditch   a very long narrow trench which is dug in the ground to drain water away

divan   a couch

dive   to plunge headfirst into water or down through the air

diver   someone who goes down into very deep water

divide   to separate into parts

dizzy   feeling that your head is spinning round and round; giddy

do   to perform or make

dock   a place where ships are unloaded or repaired

doctor   someone who helps you to get better when you are ill

dodge   to jump quickly to one side so as not to bump into something

dog   a four-legged animal which is often kept as a pet

doll   a toy made to look like a person

dome   a curved roof like half a ball

domino   a small oblong piece of wood either painted black with white dots or white with black dots. You play a game with dominoes.

donkey   an animal like a small horse with long ears

doodle   to draw or scribble while thinking about or doing something else

door   a kind of barrier which has to be opened to go in or out of a building or room. It is usually made of wood and fitted with a handle.

doorstep   the step just outside a doorway

doorway   the frame into which a door is fitted

dormitory   a big room with lots of beds

dose   the exact amount of medicine you should take at one time

dot   a small round mark

double   twice as much

doubtful   not being sure, not quite believing

dough   a thick floury mixture which is baked into bread or cakes

dove   a pretty bird, rather like a pigeon

doze   to close your eyes because you are sleepy, but not quite asleep

dozen   twelve of anything

draft   a gust of cold air

drag   to pull something heavily along the ground

dragon   an imaginary animal which breathes fire. You read about dragons in fairy stories.

dragonfly   a large flying insect with transparent wings

drain   to take away water or some other liquid

drake   a male duck

draw   to make a picture with pencils or crayons. The same word also means to pull.

drawbridge a bridge that can be let down or drawn up

drawer a kind of box that fits into a piece of furniture. It slides in and out.

drawing pin a pin with a large flat head

dread great fear

dreadful causing great fear; terrible; awful

dream the thoughts that go on in your mind after you are asleep

drench to soak right through

dress to put on clothes. The same word also means a garment worn by girls and women.

dressing gown a garment which you wear over your nightdress or pajamas

dressing table a table with a mirror where you can sit to do your hair

dressmaker a person who makes clothes for women, girls and small children

dribble to let food or liquid trickle out of the mouth on to the chin

drift to be floated or blown along

drill to bore a hole in something with a special tool. The same word also means regular practice.

drink to swallow water, milk, or some other liquid

drip to drop in little drops. A tap drips when only a little water comes out very slowly.

drive   to make something move along

driver   someone who drives

drizzle   light rain

droop   to bend or flop over

drop   to let something fall. The same word also
means a tiny bead of water.

drown   to die under water because there is no air to
breathe

drowsy   feeling very sleepy

druggist   a man who makes up medicines and sells
them, as well as things like toothpaste and
soap

drum   a hollow instrument that you beat to make
music

drumstick   the stick you use to beat a drum. The
same word also means the leg of a chicken or
turkey.

dry   not wet; without water

duck   a rather large web-footed bird which swims.
The same word also means to dip underwater
for a moment; to lower your head; to dodge
something.

due   owing; not paid

duke   a nobleman of high rank

dull uninteresting, not lively or sharp, with no sparkle

dumb not able to speak; stupid

dummy a model made to look like a person: something in place of the real thing

dump to throw down or get rid of something

dumpling a lump of flour and fat cooked in a stew

dunce a fool; someone who is slow to learn things

dungeon a dark prison cell, usually under the ground

during throughout: while something is happening

dusk the part of the evening just before the sky gets really dark

dust tiny bits of powdery dirt

duster a cloth used for wiping away dust

dustpan a container into which you sweep dust

duty what you ought to do or have to do

dwarf an animal, plant, or person who is much smaller than most others of the same kind

dye coloring powder or liquid used to change the color of cloth or other material

dynamite a powerful exploding substance

eager wanting very much to do something; keen

eagle   a large bird of prey, with a sharp curved beak and claws

ear   the part of the body you hear with. The same word means a spike of grain such as an ear of corn or barley.

earl   a nobleman of high rank

early   in good time; near the beginning

earn   to get something, usually money, in return for working: to deserve

earnest   serious; sincere

earring   jewelry which is worn on the ear

earth   the planet we live on; the world. The same word also means the ground in a garden or field.

earthquake   a violent shaking of the earth's surface

ease   freedom from pain or worry: rest from work

easel   a special stand on which a painter can put his picture while he is working on it

easily   with no difficulty

east   the direction in which the sun rises; the opposite direction to west

Easter   the time when Christians believe Jesus came back from the dead

easy   not difficult; not hard to do or understand

eat   to chew and swallow food

eaves   the edges of the roof sticking out over the top of the walls

ebb   the going back of the sea from the shore when the tide goes out

echo   a sound that comes back to you, as when you shout in a tunnel or cave

eclipse   a cutting off of light from the sun when the moon comes between the sun and the earth

edge   the cutting side of a knife. The same word also means the end of something like a table or a shelf.

educate   to help someone to learn

education   helping people to learn, usually in schools or colleges

eel   a very long fish that looks like a snake

effect   the result caused by something, as when the effect of cold weather is to make you shiver

effort   a hard try. When you use all your strength you are making an effort.

egg   an oval object with a thin shell. A chicken, like other baby birds, lives inside an egg before it is born.

eiderdown   a quilt, usually filled with feathers from an eider duck

elastic   material made with rubber which stretches easily

elbow   the joint in the middle of your arm

elder   older. The same word also means a large shrub with clusters of white blossoms which turn into purple berries later.

elderberry   a purple berry from which wine can be made

electricity   an invisible force which is used to make light and heat. It also makes power for engines and machinery.

elephant   a very large animal with a long nose called a trunk

elevator   a large metal box or cage that carries people up and down in a tall building

elsewhere   not here; somewhere else; in another place

embarrass   to make someone feel shy by teasing or by making difficulties for them

embroider   to make pretty designs on material using a needle and thread

emerald   a bright green precious stone

emperor   the male ruler of an empire

empire   a group of countries or states which is ruled by one king or queen, called an emperor or empress

employ   to give work to someone, usually for money

empress   an emperor's wife, or the female ruler of an empire

empty   with nothing or no one inside

enamel   a hard shiny paint used on such things as bathtubs, stoves, china and saucepans

enclose   to put something in an envelope or package: to surround or shut in by a fence or wall

encourage   to help someone to keep on trying; to try to give courage to someone

encyclopedia   a book or set of books which tells you something about every subject

end   the last part; the finish

endure   to bear trouble or pain with courage and patience

enemy   someone who fights against you or your country

engage   to hire someone to work for you

engaged   bound by a promise, as when a man and a woman are engaged to be married to each other

engine   a machine which makes things work. Airplanes, cars and trains are all moved by engines.

engineer   someone who makes or looks after machines. The same word also means someone who plans and builds dams, roads, railways and bridges.

enjoy   to take pleasure in something

enormous   very large; huge

enough   as much as is needed and no more

enquire   to ask. The word is also spelled inquire.

enter   to go or come into a place

entertain   to amuse. The same word also means to have someone as your guest.

entertainment   a show or concert that entertains or amuses you

enthusiasm   great interest in something; eagerness; keenness

entire   complete; whole

entrance   a doorway or way into a place

entry   the act of entering

envelope   a folded piece of paper in which you put letters for mailing

envy   a wish to have something that belongs to someone else

episode   an event in a story: a complete short story which is part of a longer story

equal   of the same size, quantity or value as something else

equator   an imaginary line around the middle of the earth's surface

equipment   all the things needed to do a job, play a game, or go on an expedition

erect   upright; standing up straight

errand   a short journey to take a message or to deliver or collect something

error   a mistake; something that has been done incorrectly

escalator   a moving staircase

escape   to get free, usually from something unpleasant

especially   most of all; of greatest importance

estimate   to guess the size, quantity or value of something

eve   evening. The same word also means the day before a special event, like Christmas Eve.

even   level; smooth. The same word also means any number that can be divided exactly by two.

evening   the time between afternoon and night

event   something that happens

ever   always; for all time

evergreen   a shrub or tree that keeps its leaves and stays green all the year round

every   each one

everybody   each person

everyday   daily. The same word also means usual or common.

everyone   another word for everybody

everything   all things

everywhere   in all places

evil   very bad; wicked; the opposite of good

ewe   a female sheep

exactly   just right; correct; with no mistakes

exaggerate   to say that something is bigger or more important than it really is

examination   a number of questions that you have to answer, usually in writing, to show how much you know about something; another word for test

examine   to look at closely and carefully

example   a sample; a single one of many. The same word also means a pattern to be copied, as when you follow somebody's good example.

excellent   very, very good

except   leaving out; apart from

exchange   to give one thing in return for another

exciting   Something which makes you feel strongly is exciting. You can feel excited if something nice is going to happen.

exclaim   to speak or call out suddenly

excuse   a reason for not doing something. It may be a good excuse or a poor excuse.

exercise   the training of your mind or body

exhaust   to use up or tire out completely. The same word also means the pipe which lets out the gases from a motor engine.

exhibition   a public show of things such as works of art, flowers, or furniture

exist   to be: to continue to live

exit   the way out of a place

expand   to grow bigger; to swell

expect   to look forward to; to think something will happen

expedition   a journey to explore a place or to search for something, such as rare plants and animals

expense   cost; payment of money

expensive   costing a lot of money; dear

experience   knowledge of something because you have seen or done it

experiment   something tried out to see what will happen: a test to find out something

expert   someone who knows a lot about a particular subject

explain   to give the meaning of something; to make something clear

explanation   anything said or written that helps you to understand clearly the reason for something

explode   to burst or blow up with a loud bang

explore   to travel to places to try to find out all about them

explosion   the act of blowing up or exploding: a sudden burst with a loud noise

express   to put thoughts into words, music or pictures. The same word also means a fast train.

expression   the look on faces when people are happy, sad, or worried. The same word also means a way of saying things.

extend   to stretch out; to make longer

extent   the length, size or area of anything

extra   more than necessary or expected

extraordinary   very unusual; not ordinary; surprising

eye   one of the two parts of your face that you see with

eyebrow   a little line of hairs over each eye

eyelash   one of the little hairs that grow along the edge of the eyelid

eyepiece   the glass part of a telescope or microscope which you look through

fable   a short story, usually about animals, which is meant to teach us a lesson

face   the front of your head

fact   a thing that everyone knows is true and not imaginary

factory   a building where things are made in large quantities, usually by machine

fade   to lose color or freshness

fahrenheit   a measurement of heat having the freezing point of water marked at 32 degrees and the boiling point at 212 degrees

fail   not to be able to do something you try to do; to be unsuccessful

failing   a fault or a bad habit

faint   pale or weak. The same word also means feeling weak and dizzy.

fair   a place where you have fun and go on rides. The same word also means light in color (as in fair hair) and right or good (as in fair play).

fairly   not bad; reasonably good

fairy   a very small person who can do magic. You read about fairies in stories for young children.

faith   what you believe in: trust that what is said is true

faithful keeping your promises; believing

fake something that looks valuable but is not; a cheap copy of something

fall to drop through the air

false wrong; not keeping your promises; not faithful; not real or true

falter to stumble; to hesitate when speaking

familiar well known or close to you

family a mother and father and their children

famine great scarcity of food; starvation

famished starving

famous well known

fan something which makes a cool breeze. The same word also means someone who is very fond of a certain sport, hobby or famous person.

fancy decorated. The same word also means imagination.

fang a long pointed tooth

far a long way away

fare the price you pay for traveling on a public vehicle such as a bus

farewell an old-fashioned word for goodbye

farm a place where a farmer keeps animals and grows food

---

farmer   a man who looks after a farm

farmyard   ground surrounded by barns, cowsheds and other farm buildings

farther   at a greater distance away; more distant

fascinating   very attractive; very charming

fast   very quick

fasten   to join together

fastening   something that fastens or closes things tightly

fat   big and round. The same word also means the whitish greasy part of meat and bacon. Other kinds of fat are found in fish and in nuts.

fatal   causing death; disastrous

father   a man who has children in his family

fault   a mistake; anything which spoils something which is otherwise good

favor   an act of kindness which is done for someone

favorite   a person or thing which is liked better than any other

fawn   a young deer

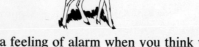

fear   a feeling of alarm when you think you are in danger

fearful   afraid. The same word also means terrible or awful.

fearless   without fear; brave

feast   a large special meal with lots of good things to eat and drink

feat   an act of great skill or strength

feather   part of the wing or the soft coat of a bird

feeble   very weak; not strong

feed   to give food to someone or some animal

feel   to find out what something is like by touching it

feet   more than one foot

fellow   a man: a companion

felt   a thick woolen material used for hats

female   people and animals who can become mothers. Girls and women are of the female sex but boys and men are of the male sex.

feminine   like, or to do with, women or girls

fence   something put round a field or garden to keep animals and people in or out

fender   a metal guard over the wheel of an automobile

fern   a plant which has lacy, feathery leaves but no flowers

ferret   a small animal used for hunting out rabbits and rats

ferry a boat used to take people or cars across water where there is no bridge

fertile able to produce seeds or plants abundantly

fester to rot; to become infected

festival a joyful celebration with dancing, music and often feasting

fetch to go and get

fête (*rhymes with gate*) an outdoor entertainment or party, usually to raise money

fever an illness which makes your body very hot and makes you feel weak and thirsty

few not many

fib a small lie; something which is not quite true

fiction a made-up story or book about people and happenings that are not really true

fiddle a violin. The same word also means to play about with something in a careless sort of way.

fiddler a man who plays a fiddle

fidget to move about in a restless way

field an open piece of land, often surrounded by hedges or fences

fierce angry; wild

fiery like fire; flaming or burning

fig a soft sweet fruit which grows on a fig tree

fight to struggle against someone or something

figure the shape of something, such as a person's body. The same word also means a number.

file a metal tool with a rough surface, used to make things smooth. The same word also means a line of people following one behind the other.

fill to put so much in a container that you cannot get any more in

film a moving picture. The same word also means a strip of material used in a camera.

filter a special strainer used to separate dirt and other solids from liquid

filthy very dirty

fin one of the wing-like parts of a fish which help it to balance and swim

final the very last; coming at the end

finally at last; at the end

find to see something you are looking for; to discover

fine excellent; very good

finger a part of your hand. You have five fingers on each hand.

fingerprint the pattern made when you press your finger or thumb on the surface of something

finish to get to the end; to complete

fir a kind of evergreen tree with leaves like needles

fire the flames, light and heat made by something burning

fire engine   a big motor vehicle that carries the firemen and their equipment to put out a fire

fireman   a man who helps to put out fires

fireplace   the open place under the chimney where a fire burns

fireside   the space next to a fireplace where you can sit and warm yourself

fireworks   Fireworks are usually made of gunpowder in a cardboard tube. They are set off after dark on special days.

firm   solid; strong and not easily moved

first   at the very beginning

fish   a swimming animal which cannot live out of water. It has fins and breathes through its gills.

fisherman   a man who catches fish

fishing   the sport or business of catching fish

fishing-net   a net used for catching fish

fishing rod   a long thin stick with a string and hook attached for catching fish

fist   a tightly closed hand

fit   to be the right size and shape for something. The same word also means in good health.

fix   to mend something. The same word also means to tie or fasten something firmly.

fizz   to bubble and make a hissing sound

flag   a piece of cloth with a colored pattern. Each country in the world has its own flag with its own pattern.

flake a very small thin piece of something, such as a snowflake

flame the bright fire that leaps from something burning

flamingo a dark pink water bird which has a long neck and long legs

flannel a soft warm woolly material

flap to move up and down, as a bird flaps its wings. The same word also means anything which hangs loose or is hinged, such as a table flap.

flare to burst into bright light, as when a piece of wood suddenly bursts into flame

flash a sudden bright light that appears only for a moment, like a flash of lightning

flask a kind of bottle, usually made of metal or glass, for holding liquids

flat smooth; without bumps and being the same height all over

flatten to make something flat

flavor what makes foods taste differently from each other. Ice cream comes in lots of flavors, like strawberry, vanilla and chocolate.

flax a plant from which strong threads can be obtained. The cloth woven from these threads is called linen.

flea a tiny jumping insect

flee to run away from something, usually because of danger

fleece the coat of wool on a sheep

fleet a number of ships or vehicles that belong together

flesh the soft parts of your body

flex to bend repeatedly

flick to hit something very lightly

flicker to burn brightly and then dimly so that the light is not steady

flight the act of flying through the air

flimsy not strong or thick, easily broken

fling to throw something away from you

flint a very hard kind of stone which gives off sparks when you strike it with steel

flit to move about very lightly and quickly

float to rest on top of a liquid or on air. A boat floats on water, and a bubble floats on air.

flock a large group of birds or of some animals

flood a great overflowing of water, usually over dry land

floor the part of a room you walk on

flop to let yourself fall down heavily

flour a white powder made from grain. It is used to make bread and cakes.

flow to move along smoothly, like water

flower the pretty colored part of a plant

flower-pot a pot in which you plant flowers

'flu a shortening of the word influenza, which is an illness causing a fever and a sore throat

fluff a light soft stuff that comes off woolen cloth and similar materials, such as blankets and carpets

fluid something that can flow, such as liquid or gas

fluke something lucky that happens by chance

flute a long thin musical instrument which you blow into

flutter to flap about; to move the wings quickly

fly to move through the air. The same word also means a flying insect.

flying fish a fish with large fins that help it to move through the air when it leaps out of the water

foal a young horse

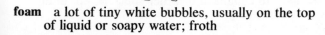

foam a lot of tiny white bubbles, usually on the top of liquid or soapy water; froth

focus to get a clear picture

foe an enemy

fog thick cloudy air

fold to double something over

foliage the leaves on trees and plants

folk people

follow to come after someone or something

folly   silliness; a foolish action

fond   loving; liking very much

font   a stone basin in a church, which contains the water for christening a baby

food   the things we eat to keep us alive

fool   a silly person

foolish   silly; stupid; not wise

foot   the part of the body you stand on. The same word also means a measure of 12 inches.

football   a team game in which you throw and kick a ball and try to score goals

footpath   a path or part of the road where people can walk but vehicles are not allowed

footprint   the mark someone's foot leaves in wet sand or soft earth

footstep   the sound a foot makes when walking

forbid   to command or order someone not to do something

force   power; strength

ford   a place in a river where the water is shallow enough for you to walk or drive through it safely

forearm   the part of your arm between your wrist and elbow

forecast   to say that something will happen before it does

forehead   the part of your face above your eyes

foreign   of another country: strange

forest   a large area of land where lots of trees are growing close together

forethought   a thought or plan for the future

forfeit   something you have to give up because of something you have done

forge   a blacksmith's workshop, with a furnace for heating the metal. The same word also means to copy someone else's handwriting for a dishonest purpose.

forgery   something written or painted which is not genuine: someone else's handwriting copied for a dishonest purpose

forget   not to remember

forget-me-not   a little blue flower

forgive   to pardon, to stop being cross with someone who has done something wrong

fork   a tool used to pick up food

form   shape. The same word also means a paper asking questions which are to be answered.

fort   a strong building made to keep enemies out

forth   onwards; out

fortnight   fourteen days; two weeks

fortress   another word for fort

fortunate   lucky

fortune   what comes by luck or chance: great riches or wealth

forward   towards the front

fossil   the remains of an animal or plant that has turned to stone after being buried for many millions of years

foul   dirty; horrible

foundations   the solid part of a building below ground level

fountain   water pushed up into the air continuously in one or more jets

fowl   a bird, usually a hen

fox   a wild animal which has a long bushy tail

fraction   a part of a whole, such as one-half ($\frac{1}{2}$) or one-third ($\frac{1}{3}$)

fragile   delicate; easily broken or damaged

fragment   a bit or piece broken off something

frame   the wood or metal around something, like a window or a picture

framework   the outline or main parts of something that the rest is built on to

fraud   dishonesty; a cheating trick

fray   a fight or quarrel

freak   a person, plant or animal whose appearance is not ordinary or normal, such as a white blackbird

freckle   a small brown spot on the skin

free   not a prisoner; able to do or say what you like. The same word also means without payment.

freeze   to become hard because of the cold, as when water turns into ice

frequent   happening often

fresh   new: healthy: not tired

fret   to be discontented; to worry

friend   someone you know well and like a lot

friendly   kind; showing friendship

frieze   a picture or pattern around the top of a wall

fright   sudden fear; alarm

frightened   afraid of something

frightful   terrible; awful

frill   an edging of lace or light material on clothing or curtains

fringe   an edging of loose threads, usually on clothing, lampshades and rugs

frisky   lively; playful

fritter   to waste something a little at a time. The same word also means a piece of meat or fruit fried in batter.

frizzy   very tightly curled

frock   a dress

frog   a small animal which lives in or near water and can jump a long way

frolic   to have fun; to dance and play games

front   the opposite to back; the most forward part of anything

frost   a thin icy covering on the ground when it is cold

froth   a lot of tiny white bubbles. usually on top of liquid; foam

frown   to wrinkle your forehead when you are angry or not pleased

frozen   solid with ice

fruit   a part of a bush or tree which can be eaten

fruitful   producing much fruit

fry   to cook something in fat or oil

frying pan   a round shallow pan for frying

fuel   anything used to make heat, such as coal, gas or wood

full   no room for any more

fully   completely; entirely

fun   to have fun is to have a good time and enjoy yourself

funeral   the ceremony of burying a dead person

funnel   a kind of chimney on a ship. The same word also means a tube that is wide at the top so that you can pour liquid into something without spilling it.

funny   amusing; laughable. Anything that makes you laugh is funny.

fur   the soft hair on animals

furnace   a place where great heat is produced by fire. Steel is made in a furnace.

furniture   the things you use in a house, such as chairs, tables and beds

furrow   a long narrow cut made in the ground by a plough

further   more distant

fury   very great anger

fuse   a piece of string or material attached to something that will explode. It burns slowly to give you time to get to safety before the explosion. The same word also means a piece of wire used for safety in an electric system.

fuss   a bother or worry, usually about something unimportant: unnecessary noise and bustle

future   the time to come: the days, months and years ahead of us

fuzzy   covered with tiny hairs or fluff. The same word also means not clear or easily seen.

gabble   to speak so quickly that people find it hard to understand what you are saying

gadget   a small cleverly designed tool or piece of apparatus

gain   to earn or win: to add to what you already have

gale   a strong wind

galleon   a large sailing ship which was used by the Spaniards hundreds of years ago

gallery   the upper floor of seats in a theater or church. The same word also means a room or building where works of art are on show.

gallon   a measure of liquid, equal to 4 quarts or 8 pints

gallop   the fastest speed at which a horse can move

galoshes   a special kind of waterproof overshoes. Sometimes the word is spelled goloshes.

gamble   to play a game for money

gambol   to skip and jump happily

game   a way of playing which has rules

gaming   another word for gambling

gander   a male goose

gang   a group of people working together. The same word also means a band of robbers or thieves.

gangster   a member of a gang of robbers and thieves

gangway   a narrow passage between rows of seats: a movable bridge between ship and shore

gantry   a bridge built over railway lines to carry signals: a support for a crane

gap   an opening or break in something

garage   a place where motor cars are kept or repaired

garden   a piece of land where flowers, fruit or vegetables are grown

garland   a circle of leaves or flowers worn on the head or around the neck or hung on something as a decoration

garment   any article of clothing

garter   a ring made of elastic which keeps a stocking from falling down

gas   something like air, neither solid nor liquid, which can fill space. It is usually invisible. Gas that burns comes through pipes and is used for cooking and heating. The same word also means a kind of liquid oil used to make motor engines work.

gash   a long deep cut or wound

gasp   to take a quick deep breath: to struggle for breath

gate   a door in a fence, wall or hedge

gather   to collect; to pick up one by one

gay   happy and lively

gaze   to stare; to look at something steadily

gear   the working part of a car or bicycle which changes the speed. The same word also means things that belong to you, such as clothes or tools.

geese   more than one goose

gem   any precious stone; a jewel

general   a commander in the army. The same word also means usual; happening everywhere.

generous   kind in sharing or giving things to others

gentle   quiet; soft or soothing

gentleman   a kind and honorable man

genuine   real; true; not a fake or copy

geography   the study of the surface of the earth and the people and animals living there

geometry   the part of mathematics to do with lines, angles and figures such as triangles and circles

geranium   a plant, usually with scarlet, white or bright pink flowers

germ   a very tiny bit of animal or plant life that you can only see under a microscope. Some germs cause diseases.

get   to receive; to fetch. The same word also means to become, as when we say someone will get well, or get rich.

ghost   the spirit of a dead person

giant   a very big strong person, usually in fairy stories

giddy   having a feeling that things are going round and round

gift   something which is given as a present

gigantic   enormous; giant-like

giggle   to laugh in a silly way

gill   an opening for breathing in a fish's skin

ginger   the root of a plant. It tastes spicy and makes your mouth feel hot.

gingerbread   a cake or biscuit which is made with ginger

giraffe   a tall animal with a very long neck

girder   a long heavy piece of metal or wood used to strengthen buildings, bridges and parts of railroads

girl   a female child; a child who will grow up to be a woman

give   to hand something over freely to someone else

glacier   a mass of ice that moves very slowly down a mountainside

glad   pleased; happy

glance   a quick look

glare   a dazzling bright light. The same word also means to stare angrily at someone.

glass   a hard material you can see through. Windows are made of glass.

glasses   two framed pieces of a special kind of glass. If you cannot see well, glasses help you to see better.

gleam   to shine, but not brightly. Old metal gleams when it is polished.

glen   a narrow valley

glide   to move smoothly and easily; to flow gently

glider   a light airplane which can fly for some time without an engine after being launched

glimmer   to shine faintly and unsteadily

glimpse   a very brief sight of someone or something

glint   to gleam or glimmer

glisten   to shine or gleam

glitter   to sparkle; to reflect light brightly

globe   a round object, like a ball or the world

gloomy   dark; dim: miserable; the opposite of cheerful

glove   a covering for the hand. It fits around each finger.

glow   to burn without flames; to give out a steady light

glue   a strong paste which sticks things together

glum   silent and sad; gloomy

glutton   a person who is greedy and eats too much

gnarled   twisted and lumpy, like the trunk of a very old tree

gnash   to grind your teeth together when you are very angry

gnat a small flying insect which stings

gnaw to wear something away by scraping at it with teeth, as when a dog gnaws at a bone

gnome a dwarf you read about in stories

go to start off or move

goal a kind of target. In football you have to kick the ball into the goal which is the space between two posts.

goat an animal rather like a sheep. It usually has horns and a little beard.

gobble to swallow food quickly without chewing it

goblet a kind of drinking cup with no handle

goblin a mischievous elf or fairy

God the Creator of everything

gold a yellow shiny metal which is worth a lot of money

golden the color of gold; made of gold

goldfish a small fish often kept as a pet. It is usually a pretty reddish-gold color.

golf a game which is played with a small white ball and a set of long-handled clubs

goloshes another way of spelling galoshes

gong a round metal disc which makes a deep ringing sound when you hit it

good right or satisfactory; kind; nice

goodbye a word said to someone who is just going away

goodness   the act of being good or kind

goods   things bought and sold

goose   a big bird, like a duck with a long neck

gooseberry   the fruit of the gooseberry bush. It is usually green with a rather hairy skin.

gorgeous   splendid; magnificent; richly colored and beautiful

gorilla   the largest kind of ape. It lives in Africa.

gosling   a young goose

gossip   chatter about other people, sometimes spiteful and unkind

govern   to rule or control

government   a group of people who have the power to make laws and decide what is best for the country

gown   a woman's dress. The same word also means a long loose-fitting robe or cloak.

grab   to seize hold of something suddenly

graceful   easy and smooth in movement; the opposite of clumsy

gracious   kind; charming

grade   a way of deciding how good something is. If one kind of apple is better than another, it will be graded higher. The same word also means a mark for school work, and where you are in school, such as Fourth Grade.

gradual happening slowly, a bit at a time

grain the seeds of some plants that are used as food. The same word also means a very small piece of something hard, like a grain of sand.

gram a very small weight, the thousandth part of a kilogram

grammar the study of the way people put words together when they speak or write

grand important; large; splendid

grandfather the father of your mother or father

grandmother the mother of your mother or father

granite a very hard rock used for buildings and for curbstones

grant to give, to allow as a favor

grape green, purple or red fruit that grows in bunches on a vine

grapefruit a round fruit like a large orange with a yellow skin and a sharp taste

graph a diagram, usually on squared paper, that shows how a series of measurements changes

grasp to seize and hold tightly

grass a low green plant which has many thin leaves and covers fields and lawns

grasshopper   a hopping, leaping insect. It makes a chirping noise by rubbing its wings or legs together.

grass-snake   a small and harmless snake

grate   a framework of iron for holding a fire in a fireplace. The same word also means to rub something, such as a piece of cheese, against a rough surface to reduce it to small particles.

grateful   giving thanks, thankful

grave   very serious. The same word also means a hole in the ground where a dead person is buried.

gravel   lots of little pebbles which can be used to make paths

gravy   the juices of cooked meat, sometimes mixed with flour to make it thicker

gray   the color of the sky when there is no sun

graze   to eat grass. The same word also means to scrape the skin.

grease   a thick oily substance; softened animal fat

great   large; big. The same word also means important or famous.

greed   a great longing to have more of something, even though you already have enough

green   the color of grass in springtime

greenhouse   a glass house where plants are grown

greet   to welcome; to speak to someone when you meet

greeting   a welcome: a kind wish often written on a birthday or Christmas card

greyhound   a very thin dog with long legs, used for racing

grief   great sadness

grieve   to be very sad about something; to be very unhappy

grim   stern, unsmiling, and often cruel

grime   dirt that sticks on and is hard to get off

grin   to smile broadly

grind   to crush something into a powder. The same word also means to rub together, like grinding your teeth.

grip   to hold on to something tightly

grit   a small piece of dirt or sand. The same word also means to grind.

groan   a deep unhappy sound of pain or sorrow

grocer   a man who sells many kinds of food and household supplies

groove   a long narrow cut hollowed out, usually in wood or metal

grope   to feel for something with your hands because you cannot see well

gross   very fat or big. The same word also means 12 dozen (144).

ground   the earth we walk on

groundsheet a waterproof sheet which you lie on when you camp

group a number of people or things together in one place

grove a small wood, a few trees

grow to get bigger

growl to make a low rumbling noise deep down in the throat. Dogs and lions growl when they are angry or afraid.

grown-up fully grown, adult

grub a soft fat new-born insect

grudge a feeling of unfriendliness or dislike for someone

gruff rough in manner; stern

grumble to find fault and say you are not satisfied

grumpy bad-tempered

grunt to make a noise like a pig

guard to look after someone or something and see that nothing harms it, or is harmed by it

guardian someone who guards or looks after someone or something

guess to answer a question without knowing for sure that it is the right answer

guest a visitor; someone you invite to your house, or to a restaurant

guidance explaining or showing the way to someone

guide someone who shows people the way. He leads and helps them.

guilt a feeling of having done something wrong

guinea pig a small furry animal with short ears and tail, often kept as a pet

guitar a musical instrument. It has strings which you pluck to make music.

gulf a very large bay that cuts into the land: a very deep hollow in the earth

gull a web-footed sea bird, usually colored gray and white

gullet a part inside your body which is like a tube. It leads from your mouth to your stomach.

gulp to take a quick deep swallow of food or air

gum sticky stuff which you use to fasten things together. The same word also means a soft sweet which you chew but don't swallow.

gun a machine which shoots bullets

gunpowder a special powder which explodes when you set light to it

gurgle to make a bubbly sound, as when water is let out of a bath

gush to rush out suddenly, as when water rushes out of a burst pipe

gust   a sudden burst or rushing out of wind or laughter

gutter   a narrow hollow for draining off rain water, usually on a roof or at the roadside

gymnasium   a large room fitted with ropes, bars and all kinds of equipment for exercise

gypsy   someone who belongs to a race of dark people who originally came from India. Gypsies wander from place to place and usually have no permanent home.

habit   something you do regularly and often, almost without thinking about it, such as brushing your teeth

haddock   a sea fish, rather like a cod

hail   frozen rain which falls as little lumps of ice

hair   the soft covering which grows on your head

hairbrush   a special brush you use for tidying and arranging your hair

hairdresser   someone who cuts and arranges people's hair

half   one of two equal parts. When you cut something in half, you divide it into two parts which are exactly the same size.

hall   the space inside the entrance of a building. The same word also means a large room used for special occasions, like a town hall.

halo   a ring of light around the sun or moon, or around the heads of holy people in paintings

halt   to stop

halve   to divide into two equal parts

hammer   a heavy tool for hitting or breaking things

hammock   a swinging bed of netting or canvas hung up by ropes at each end

hamper   a large basket with a lid, often used for carrying food. The same word also means to hinder.

hamster   a little furry animal, usually golden-brown in color. It is often kept as a pet.

hand   the end of your arm which you use to hold things

handbag   a small light bag that you can carry in your hand

handful   as much as your hand will hold; a small number or quantity

handicap   to make something more difficult for someone

handicraft   work in which things are made by hand and not by machine

handiwork   work, like sewing or clay modeling, which you do with your hands

handkerchief   a small piece of cloth for wiping your nose or eyes

handle   the part of something by which you can hold it, like the handle of a cup. The same word also means to touch or hold things with your hands.

handlebar   the part of a bicycle you hold on to and steer with

handsome   good-looking

handy   useful and clever with your hands. The same word also means near; close at hand.

hang   to fasten something to a firm support so that it swings freely, but cannot fall

hangar   a large shed for aircraft

hanger   a shaped piece of metal or wood to hang clothes on so that they don't get wrinkled

haphazard   not planned; happening just by chance

happen   to take place

happiness   joy; gladness

happy   full of joy

harbor   a sheltered place where ships stay before going out to sea

hard   not soft. Stones are hard. The same word also means difficult.

harden   to make or become hard

hardly   scarcely; only just

hardy   tough; brave

hare   an animal like a large rabbit

harm   to damage or hurt

harmful   doing harm or damage

harmless   the opposite of harmful; doing no harm

harness   the straps and other equipment worn by a horse

harp a big musical instrument shaped like a triangle. It has strings which you pluck to make music.

harpoon a sharp spear attached to a rope, used for hunting whales

harsh rough or unkind

harvest the gathering of grain and fruit

haste hurry

hasten to hurry up

hat a covering for the head

hatch to break out of the eggshell, as when baby birds and chicks are hatched

hatchet a small ax

hate to dislike someone or something very much

haughty full of pride

haul to drag along; to pull

haunt to visit a place very often

haunted lived in or visited by ghosts

have to own or to hold

havoc very great damage, as when trees are blown down in a strong wind

hawk   a bird of prey that hunts small birds and
animals

hawthorn   a kind of large bush which grows wild. It
has pink or white flowers in spring and red
berries in the autumn.

hay   dried grass used for feeding animals

haze   mist or thin cloud

hazel   a small nut tree

head   the part of your body above your neck. The
same word also means a person who is in
charge; a chief or leader.

head dress   something very decorative worn on the
head on special occasions or as part of a
costume

heal   to make someone well again

health   how your body feels. You have good health
when you are not ill.

healthy   well in body and mind; free from illness

heap   a pile, like a heap of dead leaves

hear   to use your ears to listen to sounds

heart   the part of your body which pumps the blood
around inside you

hearth   the floor of a fireplace

heat   to make something hot

heater   something that produces heat, such as an electric fire

heave   to haul or lift something up with a great effort

heaven   the home of God. The same word also sometimes means the sky.

heavy   difficult to pick up and carry away; weighing a lot

hedge   lots of bushes growing close together in a line, like a fence

hedgehog   a little animal with a coat like sharp needles mixed with hair

heel   the back of your foot. The same word also means the back part of your shoe.

height   how tall or high something is

heir   a man or boy who will receive money, property, or a title when the present owner dies

heiress   a woman or girl who will receive money, property, or a title when the present owner dies

helicopter   a kind of aircraft without wings which can go straight up or down in the air as well as straight ahead

hell   a place of misery

helmet   a covering, usually made of metal, which protects the head. Soldiers, racing-drivers, and motorbike riders wear them.

help   to make something easier for a person to do. You help your mother to wash the dishes.

helpful   being of help

helpless   not able to help yourself or others, often because of weakness

hem   an edge of cloth which is folded over and sewn to make it neat

hen   a mother bird

herb   a plant which is used for flavoring food or for medicine

herd   a group of animals kept together, such as a herd of cows

here   in this place

hero   a man or boy who does something brave. The same word also means the most important man in a book or play.

heroine   a girl or woman who does something brave. The same word also means the most important woman in a book or play.

heroism   great bravery

herring   a small seafish

herself   she and no one else

hesitate   to pause because you are not sure what to do or to say next

hibernate   to sleep all through the winter, as some
        animals do

hiccup   to make a sharp noise in your throat,
        usually when you have eaten or drunk too
        quickly. Sometimes the word is spelled
        hiccough.

hide   to go where no one can see you or to put
        something where no one can see it. The
        same word also means the skin of
        an animal.

hide-and-seek   a game where one person hides and
        another tries to find him

hideous   very ugly; horrible

hiding   a beating or whipping

high   a long way up. Mountains are high.

highway   a public road

highwayman   a robber on horseback who held up
        travelers on the road in olden days

hill   part of the ground that is higher than the rest,
        but lower than a mountain

himself   he and no one else

hinder   to delay or prevent someone from doing
        something

hinge   a joint, usually of metal. Doors are fitted
        with hinges so that they can be opened
        and shut.

hint   to suggest something without actually saying it
        in so many words. You might say to someone
        that it is getting late as a hint that you wish
        he would go home.

hip   one of the sides of your body just below your waist

hippopotamus   a very big animal which lives in hot countries

hire   to pay for the use of something for a certain length of time. You can hire a taxi. The same word also means to employ.

hiss   to make a noise that sounds like s-s-s-s-s. Snakes and geese make hissing sounds.

history   the study of what has happened in the world in the past

hit   to knock something. The same word also sometimes means a show or a tune which is a big success.

hive   a house for bees

hoard   a store or stock of something hidden away. Squirrels have a hoard of nuts hidden away for the winter.

hoarse   having a rough-sounding voice, as when you have a sore throat

hob   a place near the hearth where things can be kept hot

hobble   to walk with difficulty because you are lame

hobby   something you very much like to do in your spare time, such as collecting stamps or making models

hockey   a team game where you try to hit a ball into the goal with a long stick curved at one end.

Sometimes the game is played on ice, with a rubber disc instead of a ball.

hoe   a long-handled garden tool for clearing weeds and loosening the earth

hold   to have in your hand or your arms; to contain. The same word also means the part of a ship where cargo is kept.

hole   an opening in or through something

holiday   a time when you do not have to work or go to school

hollow   having a space or a hole inside: a valley

holly   a tree with evergreen prickly leaves and bright red berries. It is often used for decoration at Christmas.

hollyhock   a tall plant with many large flowers on each stalk

holster   a leather case on a belt for holding a gun

holy   anything specially belonging to, or to do with God

home   the place where you live

homework   work done at home, usually school work

honest   truthful; not likely to steal from others

honey   a sweet food which is made by bees

honk   the loud cry of a wild goose: the noise of an automobile horn

honor   to show respect for someone or something

hood   a loose cloth covering for the head. It is sometimes fastened to a coat or jacket.

hoof   the hard part of a horse's foot. Cattle, deer and some other animals also have hooves.

hook   a curved pointed piece of metal for catching, holding, or pulling things

hooligan   a rough noisy person who goes about the streets bullying people and damaging property

hoop   a large ring made of metal or wood

hoot   to shout scornfully at someone. The same word also means the cry of an owl at night; the sound of a motor horn.

hop   to jump on one leg or move in short jumps

hope   to wish that something may happen, although you know it may not

hopeful   hoping; full of hope

hopeless   without hope; impossible

horde   a crowd or mass of people

horizon   the place where the sky and earth appear to meet

horn   one of the hard sharp bony parts that grow out of the heads of some animals such as cows and goats. The same word also means a musical instrument that you blow.

horrible   dreadful; ugly and awful

horrid   nasty; very unpleasant

horror   a very great fear or loathing

horse   an animal used for riding
and for pulling carts,
coaches and carriages

horseback   on the back of a horse

horse chestnut   a kind of chestnut tree. It has
cone-shaped bunches of white or pink flowers
in spring and shiny brown nuts inside prickly
coverings.

horseshoe   a curved iron shoe which is nailed to the
bottom of a horse's hoof

hose   a long thin tube used for carrying water from
a tap. The same word also means socks or
stockings.

hospital   a place where people who are ill or hurt
are looked after by doctors and nurses

host   a boy or man who has other people as his
guests: an old fashioned word for innkeeper.
The same word sometimes means a crowd or a
large number.

hostess   a girl or woman who has other people as
her guests

hot   very warm

hotel   a building with many rooms, where you pay
for a bedroom and food when you are traveling

hound   a hunting dog

hour   60 minutes

house   a building to live in

houseboat   a large flat-bottomed boat used as a
floating house

household   all the people who live in the same house

hover   to float or stay in one place in the air

hovercraft   a vehicle without wheels that can glide very quickly over the earth's surface, both land and water

how   in what way

howl   to make a long loud whining noise

hub   the middle of a wheel

huddle   crowded closely together, sometimes to keep warm

hug   to hold someone or something close to you in your arms

huge   enormous; very big

hull   the main part of a ship

hum   to make a musical sound in your nose as though you are saying m-m-m-m without opening your mouth

human   a man, woman or child. The same word also means having to do with people, not with other animals or plants.

humble   the opposite of proud or boasting, meek

humid   moist, damp

humor   fun; jokes

humorist   someone who makes you laugh at his jokes and sayings

humorous   funny; amusing

hump   a lump or large bump, often on the back of an animal, like a camel's hump

hunger   a need for food

hungry   feeling you want something to eat

hunt   to chase after something which you want to catch

hunter   someone who hunts wild animals or birds for food or sport

hurdle   a kind of wooden fence which animals or people have to jump over in some races

hurl   to throw something away from you with all your strength

hurricane   a very great windstorm

hurry   to move fast in order to get somewhere more quickly, or to finish what you are doing sooner

hurt   to give pain

hurtle   to rush or dash with great force and speed

husband   a married man

hush   to become quiet or silent

hustle   to hurry; to make someone hurry along by pushing and shoving

hut   a small wooden house

hutch   a little wooden house for a pet rabbit

hyacinth   a spring flower which has spikes of bright, sweet-smelling blossoms

hyena   a wild animal rather like a dog. It makes a high laughing sound and lives in some hot countries.

hymn   a song which praises God

ice   water which has been frozen hard by the cold

ice cream   a frozen food made with milk and sugar

icicle   a long thin spike of ice, usually hanging from a roof

icing   a sugar coating for cakes

idea   a plan which you think of, or a picture in your mind

ideal   perfect; exactly right

idiot   a person whose mind does not work properly; a crazy person

idle   lazy; not working; doing nothing

idol   an image or statue of a person or animal that is worshipped as a god

igloo   a hut made of blocks of hard snow. It has a domed roof.

ignorant   without knowledge; not knowing

ignore   to take no notice; to pretend someone or something is not there

ill   not well; not healthy

illuminate   to light or throw light upon

illustration   a picture, usually in a book. The same

word also means an example that helps to explain something.

image an exact likeness or copy of something; a statue

imaginary something you think of that is not real

imagine to picture in your mind what something or someone is like

imitate to copy, to do something the same as someone else

immediately at once

immense enormous; very big

imp a little devil: a naughty child

important of great interest or value. The same word also means powerful.

impossible not able to be done

impress to make something stick in someone's mind

impression an idea or thought that is fixed firmly in your mind. The same word also means a mark that is made by pressing or printing.

impressive making a deep impression on the mind

improve to make better; to become better

impudent not respectful

inch a measure of length. There are 12 inches in one foot.

incident something that happens; an event

include to count something in; to contain

increase   to get bigger or more in number

index   a list in alphabetical order, usually at the end of a book. It shows the numbers of the pages where things are mentioned in the book.

indignant   annoyed or angry about something you think is wrong

indigo   a purplish-blue color; a dye of that color

indoors   inside a building; the opposite of outdoors

industry   hard work. The same word also means making things in factories.

infant   a baby; a young child

infirmary   another name for a hospital

inflammable   easily set on fire

inform   to tell or give information

information   facts told to someone or given in a book; knowledge

infuriate   to make very angry

inhabit   to live in or occupy

initial   the first letter of a word or name

injection   a prick, usually in the arm with a hollow needle. Through the needle a liquid medicine is pushed into your bloodstream to make you better, or to stop you from getting an illness.

injure   to harm or hurt

injury   a hurt or wound

ink   a colored liquid used with a pen for writing

inn   a small hotel where travelers can stay, and where they can buy food and drink

innocent   without guilt

inquire   to ask. This word can also be spelled enquire.

inquiry   a question; a seeking of information. This word can also be spelled enquiry.

inquisitive   eager to find out about something; curious; nosey

insect   a very small animal with six legs. Ants, bees and beetles are insects.

inside   within; not outside

insist   to demand; to say or ask over and over again

inspect   to look carefully at something; to examine

inspector   someone who examines things to make sure everything is all right. The same word also means a policeman who is in charge of other policemen.

installment   one of the parts of a serial story or film; one part of the money owed for something you pay for bit by bit

instantly   at once; without delay

instead   in place of

instinct   an ability to do things without being taught. Baby ducks are able to swim by instinct.

instruct   to teach or inform someone

instrument   a tool. The same word also means something which makes music.

insult to say something rude or hurtful

intelligent brainy; clever at learning

intend to mean to do something, as when you intend to pay someone back

intense very great

interest a wish to know more about something

interesting attracting or holding your interest

interfere to meddle; to hinder; to try to stop something from going on

interrupt to break in on something which is happening, like starting to speak when someone is already speaking

interval a period of time between two events, such as a ten-minute interval between two acts in a play

interview a talk with someone, often broadcast or reported in a newspaper

introduce to tell people each other's names when they meet for the first time. The same word also means to bring a new idea into what you are talking about or doing.

invade to go into a place by force, as when an army invades the enemy's country in wartime

invalid a person who is ill

invent to think up, or make something which is completely new and has never been thought of or made before

invisible not able to be seen

invite   to ask someone to come to your home or to go somewhere with you

iris   the colored part of the eye. The same word also means a garden plant with large flowers and sword-shaped leaves.

iron   a strong gray metal. The same word also means a tool that takes the wrinkles out of clothes.

irritate   to annoy or make angry. The same word also means to itch.

island   a piece of land with water all around it

isle   another word for island

issue   a result; a problem. The same word also means to send or give something out.

italics   a kind of lettering that slants to the right, *as these words do*

itch   a tickling feeling on your skin which makes you want to scratch

ivy   an evergreen climbing plant

jab   to poke or stab at something suddenly

jackal   a wild animal that looks like a dog

jacket   a short coat. The same word means a loose paper cover on a book.

jagged   having sharp and rough edges

jaguar a fierce wild animal, rather like a leopard

jail another word for prison

jam fruit cooked together with sugar until it is thick and soft

jar a pottery or glass container with a wide opening

jaw one of the two large bones your teeth grow in

jazz a kind of lively dance music

jealous wishing you had something someone else has; full of envy

jeans trousers made of a strong cotton cloth

jeep a small open motor vehicle used by the army

jeer to make fun of someone in an unkind way

jelly a transparent wobbly food, usually fruit-flavored

jerk a short sudden movement

jersey a tight-fitting knitted sweater with sleeves

jest to say something to make people laugh; to joke

jet a rush of liquid or gas through a small opening in a pipe or hose. The same word also means a kind of airplane without propellers.

jetty a small pier

jewel a valuable stone, like a diamond or emerald

jewelry necklaces, bracelets, rings, brooches and other ornaments made of jewels and precious metals, such as gold and silver

jib the small triangular sail at the front of a sailboat

jig a jolly dance

jigsaw a fine saw that can cut wood or cardboard into small curved and straight pieces

jigsaw puzzle a puzzle made of odd-shaped pieces cut by a jigsaw. You have to put them together to make a picture.

jingle a clinking tinkling sound made by coins or bells

job work done, usually for money

jockey a boy or man who rides a horse in a race

jog to move along more quickly than walking, but not so fast as running. The same word also means to give a little push, as when you jog someone's elbow.

join to put together or fasten. The same word also means to become a member of a group, such as a club or a choir.

joint the place where two parts of something grow or are joined together

joke something a person says or does to make you laugh

jolly   cheerful; full of fun

jolt   to move forward in jerky movements. The same word also means a bump or shaking-up.

jostle   to push or knock against someone, usually in a crowd

journal   another word for a magazine or newspaper. The same word also means a diary.

journey   a trip. When you travel from one place to another you make a journey.

jovial   cheerful; jolly

joy   a feeling of great happiness

judge   the person in authority in a court of law who decides how someone who has done wrong should be punished

jug   a container with a handle, used for pouring milk and other liquids

juggler   someone who is very clever at balancing things and keeping them moving in the air

juice   liquid in oranges, lemons, tomatoes and other fruit and vegetables

juke-box   an instrument that plays records when you put money in it

jumble   a mixture of odd things

jump   to spring up off the ground

jumper   a dress without sleeves worn over a blouse or sweater

junction   a place where railroad lines or roads meet

jungle   a forest in hot countries where plants and

trees grow so thickly that it is hard to find your way through

junior   someone who is younger or less important than others

junk   something of no use or value; rubbish. The same word also means a Chinese sailing ship.

jut   to stick out

kaleidoscope   a toy shaped like a tube, with small pieces of colored glass which change patterns when you turn the tube round

kangaroo   an animal which can jump a long way. It has a pocket for its babies.

keel   a heavy piece of wood or metal that goes along the bottom of a boat or ship from one end to the other

keen   having a fine, sharp cutting edge or point; very interested in something

keep   to hold on to something and not give it away. The same word also means the strongest, inside part of a castle.

keeper   someone who looks after or guards something, like a gamekeeper or a keeper at the zoo

kennel   a small house or shelter for a dog

kernel   the inside part of a nut that can usually be eaten

kettle   a metal container used for boiling water. It has a lid, a handle and a spout.

key   a small piece of metal, specially shaped so that it will open a lock. The same word also means a lever on a piano or typewriter.

keyboard   the keys of a piano, organ or typewriter, arranged in order

keyhole   a hole specially shaped so you can put a key in it

kick   to hit something or someone with your foot

kid   a young goat. The same word also means a child.

kidnap   to take someone away by force

kill   to cause someone or something to die

kilogram   a unit of weight, equal to 1,000 grams

kilometer   a unit of length, equal to 1,000 meters

kilt   a short pleated skirt with a tartan pattern

kimono   a loose garment, usually fastened with a sash

kind   friendly; good to other people. The same word also means sort or type.

kindergarten   a school or class for very young children

king   a man who rules a country usually because his family did so before him

kingdom a country ruled by a king or queen

kipper a herring that has been salted and then dried in a special kind of smoke

kiss to touch with your lips someone or something you like

kit all the gear needed for something, such as a tool kit; a complete outfit

kitchen a room where cooking is done

kite a toy made of paper or cloth on light wood. It can be flown on the end of a string when it is windy.

kitten a young cat

knapsack a bag for food and clothes that you carry on your back

knave a man who is not honest

knee the joint in the middle of your leg

kneel to get down on your knees; to rest on your knees

knife a thin sharp piece of metal with a handle, used for cutting

knight a nobleman. In the old days, he used to dress in armor and fight for his king.

knit to weave wool into clothing with long needles

knob a round handle, like a door knob

knock to hit something hard or to bump into something

knocker a thick piece of metal fastened to a door
by a hinge. When you lift it and then let it
drop, it makes a loud noise.

knot the place where two pieces of string or ribbon
have been tied together

know to understand and be sure about something
you have read or seen

knowledge what you have learned and understand
about things

knuckle a finger joint

label a small piece of paper or cardboard with
writing or printing on it. You stick labels on
such things as jars, boxes or luggage, so that
you know what is inside.

laboratory a room or building where scientific tests
are carried out

labor hard work

lace a string used to fasten shoes. The same word
also means material with a pretty pattern of
holes.

lack to be in need of something you haven't got. If
you are hungry, you lack food.

lad a boy

ladder a set of wooden or metal rungs between two
long pieces of wood or metal, used for climbing
up or down

ladle a spoon shaped like a small cup with a long
straight handle, used for serving soup or other
liquids

lady another word for a woman

ladybird a tiny flying beetle, usually red with black spots

lag to follow along slowly behind others

lair a wild beast's den

lake a very large pool of water with land all around it

lamb a young sheep

lame not able to walk easily because you have hurt your leg or your foot

lamp a light, usually in a glass container, like an electric light bulb

lance a long spear. The same word also means to cut open a boil so that the fluid can drain away.

land the parts of the earth that are not covered by water. The same word also means to come down from the air on to land or water.

landing coming back to land from the sea or air. The same word also means the floor at the top of the stairs.

landlady a woman who owns a house or apartment where other people pay to live

landlord a man who owns a house or apartment where other people pay to live

lane a little road, usually in the country

language human speech or writing. The same word also means the speech used in different countries, such as the English language and the French language.

lantern a metal and glass container for a candle or oil light. You can carry it about.

lap the top part of your legs when you are sitting down. The same word also means once around a racetrack.

larch a tree which has cones and long thin leaves like needles

lard fat from pigs, used in cooking

larder a room or cupboard where food is kept

large very big

lark a small songbird. The same word also means a frolic.

lash to hit someone with a whip: to tie up firmly

lass a girl

lasso a long rope with a sliding loop at the end. It is used to catch wild horses and cattle.

last coming at the end; after all others

latch a wood or metal fastening for a door or gate

late behind time; not early

lathe a machine for cutting and shaping pieces of wood and metal while they are being turned round

lather a foam made by using soap and water together

laugh   to make a noise to show you feel happy or think something is funny

launch   to start something on its way, such as launching a ship into the water, or a rocket into the air. The same word also means a large open motorboat.

laundry   a place where dirty clothes are washed

lavatory   a place where there is a washbasin or a toilet, sometimes both together

lavender   a plant with lavender or purple flowers that are dried and used to make linen and clothing smell sweet

law   rules made by the government of a country

lawn   a smooth flat area of grass which is cut and looked after carefully

lawnmower   a machine that is used to cut the grass on a lawn

lay   to put something down

layer   a flat covering or thickness. You put jam and cream between two layers of sponge cake.

lazy   not wanting to work or make any effort

lead (*rhymes with seed*)   to be first, before everyone else

lead (*rhymes with bed*)   a heavy soft gray metal

leader   someone who is in front or at the head of a group of people

leaf   the flat, green part of a plant or tree

leak   the accidental escape of liquid or gas from a hole or crack in a pipe or container

lean thin; without fat. The same word also means to rest against something, so that you are not standing up straight.

leap to jump high in the air

leap year a year with 366 days, having 29 days in February. It comes every four years.

learn to find out about things or how to do something

least the smallest in size or importance

leather the skin of animals, used to make things like shoes and gloves

leave to go away from somewhere. The same word also means to let something stay where it is.

lecture a talk given to an audience or a class at school

ledge a narrow shelf

leek a vegetable with long green leaves and a thick white stem, tasting something like an onion

leer to smile at someone in a nasty way

left the opposite side to right. You have a right hand and a left hand.

leg the part of your body which joins on to your foot. You have two legs. The same word also means one of the pieces of wood that hold up a table or chair.

legend a story from long ago which may or may not be true

legion a large group of soldiers: a large number

lemon a sour yellow fruit

lemonade a drink made from lemon juice and sugar

lend to let someone have something of yours which he will give back to you

length how long something is

lengthen to make longer

lens a curved piece of glass used in eye glasses or in instruments such as telescopes and cameras

leopard a dangerous wild animal that looks like a large cat with spots

lesson something to be learned

let to agree that someone may do something; to give permission

letter how a sound looks when it is written down. Our alphabet has 26 letters. The same word also means a written message that is put in an envelope.

lettuce a garden plant with large green leaves which you can eat without cooking

level another word for flat; with no bumps

lever a bar pushed down at one end so that it lifts something on the other end

liar someone who tells lies

liberty freedom to do as you think is right

library a room or building full of books

license   a special piece of printed paper that you must have before you can do certain things. You need a license to own a gun or to drive a car.

lick   to touch something with your tongue, like a lollipop or an ice cream

licorice   black chewy sweets made from sugar mixed with the root of a plant

lid   the top which can be taken off something, such as a box or saucepan

lie   to say something that you know is not true. The same word also means to rest flat.

life   the time between your birth and your death

lifeboat   a special boat kept ready to rescue people who have been shipwrecked

lift   to move or raise something up

light   not heavy. The same word also means something which shines brightly so that you can see in the dark.

lighten   to make less heavy or less dark

lighter   something used to produce fire, like a cigarette lighter

lighthouse   a tower with a strong light to guide ships at sea in the dark

lightly   gently; not heavily

lightning   a sudden bright flash of light in the sky when there is a thunderstorm

like   to be fond of or be pleased with. The same word also means the same or almost the same.

likeable pleasant; easy to get on with. Sometimes the word is spelled likable.

likely probable; expected to happen

likeness something that looks the same as the real thing

lilac a large garden bush with sweet-smelling white or purple flowers in the spring

lily a tall garden plant with large white or brightly-colored flowers

limb an arm or leg: a branch

lime white powder made from limestone, used for making cement. The same word also means a green-colored sour fruit, something like a small lemon.

limit the place where something ends

limp without stiffness, like wilted flowers. The same word also means to walk in a lame way.

line a thin mark like this _____

linen cloth made from the flax plant. The same word also means sheets, pillowcases, towels and other household linen.

liner a large ship that carries people and cargoes long distances

linger to loiter; to delay leaving

link one of the rings in a chain

linoleum   a stiff shiny floor covering

lint   soft woolly material used to protect sores or wounds

lion   a strong and dangerous wild animal, like a very big cat

lioness   a female lion

lips   the soft edges of the mouth

lipstick   a kind of crayon in a case, used by girls and women to color their lips red or pink

liquid   anything which is wet and flows like water

list   words placed underneath each other in a column, like a shopping list or a list of names

listen   to try to hear something

liter   a measurement of capacity

literature   poems, stories and books

litter   rubbish or waste paper left lying about. The same word also means all the babies born to a mother animal at one time.

little   not big; small

live (*rhymes with give*)   to have life; to be alive

live (*rhymes with five*)   living; not dead; alive

lively   jolly; active; full of life

liver   an inside part of the body

living room a room with comfortable furniture where the family gathers together to talk, read, watch television or entertain visitors

lizard a scaly reptile with four legs

llama a large animal with a long woolly coat, something like a camel without any humps

load all that can be carried at one time, like a load of bricks or a load of bananas. The same word also means to put bullets into a gun, ready for shooting.

loaf a large piece of bread with crust all over it

loan something you lend to someone for a while

loathe to hate or despise greatly

lob a stroke in tennis when the ball goes high in the air

lobby the entrance hall in a large building

lobster a shellfish with two large strong claws

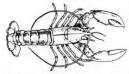

local nearby; near or close by a certain place

lock a strong fastening for a door or gate that can only be opened with a key

locomotive a railway engine

locust an insect something like a large grasshopper, that destroys crops

lodge a small house at the entrance to a park or at the gates of a large house in the country

lodger   someone who pays to live in someone else's house

loft   space under the roof which can be used as a store room

log   a thick round piece of wood. The same word also means a ship's diary.

loiter   to linger; to dawdle

loll   to sit or lie about in a lazy way

lollipop   a large sweet on the end of a stick

lone   the only one

lonely   feeling sad because you are alone

long   a big distance from one end to the other

look   to watch or try to see

looking glass   another word for mirror

loom   a machine for weaving thread into cloth

loop   a ring of wire, string or ribbon

loose   the opposite of tight; not properly fastened

loosen   to make something less tight

lord   an important nobleman

lose   not to be able to find something

lot   a large number; a great many

lotion   a soothing liquid medicine that you put on sore places on your skin

lotus   a waterlily that grows in some hot countries

loud   noisy; easily heard

loudspeaker   an instrument that makes sounds louder, so that you can hear them from a distance

lounge   a room with comfortable chairs in a club, hotel or house. The same word also means to loll or lie about in a lazy way.

lovable   worth loving

love   to be very fond of, to like someone or something very much

lovely   beautiful or pretty; nice

low   not high or tall

loyal   faithful; true to someone

luck   something that happens by chance. You can have good luck or bad luck.

lucky   having good luck

luggage   the cases, trunks or bags you take your clothes in when you travel

lukewarm   in between warm and cool

lumber   timber sawed into boards or planks of standard length. The same word also means to walk in a heavy, clumsy way.

lump   a piece of something, usually without any special shape, like a lump of clay or dough

lunar   having to do with the moon

lunch   the meal eaten at midday. The word is short for luncheon.

lunge   to make a sudden thrust or rush at something

lurch   to jerk forward on to one side

lurk   to hide yourself while you are waiting about for someone or something

luscious   delicious

luxury   something expensive and pleasant that you would like to have but don't really need: great comfort

macaroni   long stiff tubes of dried wheat paste that become soft when cooked in boiling water

macaw   a brilliantly colored large parrot with a long tail and harsh cry

machine   an instrument, usually made of metal, which does a job of work, like a sewing machine or a washing machine

machine gun   a gun that fires bullets quickly, one after the other, without stopping

machinery   the working parts of machines; another name for machines

mackerel   a seafish caught for food. It is green with wavy markings of blue and black.

mackinaw   a short, warm coat made of thick cloth, often with a plaid pattern

mad   crazy; not right in the head. Someone who is mad does not think properly, because his mind is ill. The same word also means angry.

magazine   a thin book which comes out every week or month. It has different stories and pictures in it each time.

maggot   a tiny worm or grub that is found in bad meat, cheese or fruit

magic   an imaginary power that makes wonderful things happen that seem impossible, like changing a pumpkin into a beautiful coach

magician   someone who can do magic

magnet   a piece of iron or steel that has the power to pull other pieces of metal to it

magnificent   splendid; very grand

magpie   a black and white bird of the crow family. It is noisy and likes to collect bright shiny objects.

maid   an old-fashioned word for a girl or young woman. The same word is also used for a woman servant.

mail   anything that is sent through the post, such as letters and parcels

main   most important; chief

majesty   a title given to a king or queen

major   of great importance. The same word also means an officer in the army.

make   to produce, to build

make-up   face powder, lipstick and coloring used around the eyes

male   people and animals who can become fathers. Boys and men are of the male sex, but girls and women are of the female sex.

malt   grain prepared in a special way before it is made into beer

mammal   one of any kind of animal whose females have milk to feed their babies

mammoth   huge; enormous. The same word also means a huge hairy elephant that lived millions of years ago.

man   a male human being when he is grown up

manage   to look after or be responsible for something, such as a business or a household

manager   a person who is in charge of something, such as a business, a football club or a factory

mane   the long hair some animals have on their necks. Horses have manes and so do lions.

manger   a feeding box for animals, usually in a shed or stable

mangle   to destroy by battering, cutting or tearing

mankind   all human beings

manners   how you behave towards other people, the way in which you do things. It is good manners to say please and thank you, but bad manners to snatch things and act in a rude way.

manor   the land belonging to a nobleman

mansion   a very large house

mantelpiece   a narrow shelf above the fireplace

manure   anything put into the ground to make plants and crops grow better

many   a lot

map   a special kind of drawing to show how to find your way about a place, a country or the different parts of the world

marble   a hard kind of stone that is used in important buildings. Marble is also carved into statues and beautiful ornaments. The same word also means one of the round glass balls used in the game of marbles.

march   to walk in step. Soldiers march in time to music in a parade.

mare   a female horse

margarine   a soft yellow food that looks like butter

margin   a blank edge on the side of a page where nothing is printed

marigold   a bright yellow or orange garden flower

marine   to do with the sea. The same word also means a soldier serving on a ship.

marionette   a puppet made to move by pulling strings

mark   a spot or line on something

market   a place, sometimes out of doors, where people meet to buy and sell food and other things

marmalade   a kind of jam made from oranges, lemons or grapefruit cooked with sugar

maroon   a dark brownish-red color

marriage   the ceremony by which a man and woman become husband and wife

marry   to become husband and wife

marsh   a piece of wet swampy land which is unsafe to walk on because your feet sink down into it

marshal   in some countries, an important officer in the army. The same word also means a sheriff.

marshmallow   a soft sticky white or pink sweet

marshy   wet; swampy

marvel   to wonder; to be amazed

marvelous   wonderful; splendid

marzipan   a sweet food made of crushed almonds and sugar

mascot   a person or animal or charm that is supposed to bring good luck

masculine   like, or to do with, men or boys

mash   to crush something so that it becomes soft and smooth, like mashed potatoes

mask   a cover to hide the face, sometimes funny, sometimes pretty and sometimes frightening

mass   a lump of something; a large quantity or number

massive   large and heavy

mast   a long pole that holds up the sails of a sailing vessel

master   someone who is in control or in command of other people

mat   a piece of thick material on a floor. Small mats are used on tables under hot plates.

match a small thin piece of wood or cardboard with a tip that makes fire

mate a friend or helper; someone you often play or work with; a husband or wife

material what anything is made of

mathematics the study of numbers, measurements and quantities

matinée (*say matinay*) an afternoon performance of a show

mattress the thick soft part of the bed that you lie on

mauve a pale purple color

maybe another word for perhaps or possibly

mayor a man chosen to be leader of a town, city or village

maypole a high pole set up on the first day of May. The pole is decorated with flowers and ribbons, and people dance around it.

maze a place with lots of paths that cross and turn into each other so that it is hard to find your way out

meadow a field of grass, often made into hay and used to feed animals

meal food eaten at certain times of the day. Breakfast, lunch, dinner and supper are all meals.

mean selfish and unkind. The same word is also used for explaining things, such as that the word *mean* means selfish and unkind.

meaning the sense or explanation of something said or written

meanwhile the time between two events or happenings

measles an illness. You have a high fever and are covered in small itchy red spots.

measure to find out the size or amount of anything

measurement the size or amount of something

meat the parts of animals that are cooked and eaten

mechanical machine-like. A mechanical toy is worked by machinery, not by a person.

medal a piece of metal like a coin or cross hanging on a ribbon. It is given as a reward for being very brave or very skillful.

meddle to interfere with what someone else is trying to do

medicine something that you eat or drink or rub on yourself to make you feel better when you are ill

medium middle-sized

meek gentle and patient; not likely to fight back or lose your temper easily

meet to come together with someone or something

meeting coming together for a purpose

melt to turn to liquid when heated. Butter melts in warm weather and so does ice.

member someone who belongs to a team or club or some other group of people

memory the part of your mind that remembers things

men more than one man

mend to make something right; to repair it when it is torn or broken

mental to do with the mind: worked out in your head and not written out

mention to speak briefly about something

menu a piece of card or paper with a list of what there is to eat in a restaurant or café

mercy pity; forgiveness

meringue (*say merang*) a white crisp food made from white of egg and sugar, whipped stiff and then baked in an oven

merit to deserve something, such as a reward or punishment

mermaid an imaginary sea creature, supposed to be half woman and half fish, with a fish tail instead of legs

merry happy; enjoying yourself

merry-go-round a machine at the fair which you can ride on as it goes round and round

mess an untidy muddle; confusion

message   something you want a person who is not with you to know, so you write it down or ask another person to tell him

messenger   someone who carries a message

metal   hard materials like iron and steel. Cars and airplanes are mostly made of metal.

meteor   a piece of rock traveling in space, often called a shooting star

meter   an instrument for measuring a quantity of something, such as gas, water or electricity. The same word also means a measure of length equal to 100 centimeters.

method   a way of doing something

mew   the crying sound made by a cat or kitten

mice   more than one mouse

microphone   an instrument that picks up sounds for radio, television or tape recorders

microscope   an instrument with a tube that you look through, which makes very tiny things look much larger

midday   the middle of the day between morning and afternoon

middle   halfway; in the center

midget   a person who is very small, even when grown up

midnight   12 o'clock at night, the middle of the night

midst   another word for middle, when you mean in the middle of a crowd of people

mighty   another word for powerful or strong

mild   not strong or severe

mile   a measure of distance equal to 1,760 yards or 5,280 feet

milk   the white liquid that is used to feed babies. Most people drink cow's milk.

milkman   a man who sells milk, or brings milk to your house

mill   a machine for grinding things like grain, coffee beans and pepper into very small pieces. The same word also means a building or factory where cloth or steel is made.

millimeter   a thousandth part of a meter

million   a thousand times a thousand; 1,000,000

millionaire   a very rich man who has a million dollars or more

mimic   to imitate or copy someone else, usually in a mocking way

mince   to chop or grind something, usually meat, into very small pieces

mincemeat   a mixture of chopped-up fruit, nuts, raisins and other things, cooked in pastry, usually at Christmas time

mind   what you think with. The same word also means to be careful in what you are doing.

mine   a large deep hole in the ground where men dig for coal, diamonds, gold or other minerals. The same word also means belonging to me.

miner a man who works in a mine

mineral any substance in the earth that can be dug out and used, such as coal, metal, rock

mingle to mix with or go about with, as when you mingle with the crowd at a football game

miniature a small copy of anything

minor not important. The same word also means a person who is not yet an adult.

mint a place where coins are made. The same word also means a small garden plant used for flavoring sauces and sweets.

minute One minute is 60 seconds. It takes 60 minutes to make an hour.

miracle something wonderful or fortunate that you would not expect to happen

mirage something you imagine you can see that is not really there, as when hot and thirsty travelers in the desert think they see water ahead

mirror a piece of glass with something behind it so that you can see yourself instead of seeing through the glass

misbehave to behave badly or in a rude way

mischief harm or damage; naughtiness

miser someone who hoards all his money and lives in a very poor way

miserable feeling very sad and unhappy

misery unhappiness; sorrow

misfortune bad luck; a calamity

miss to fail to hit, catch or find something

mist very low cloud

mistake something wrong, like a mistake in your arithmetic

mistletoe an evergreen plant with pearly-looking berries, which grows on the branches of trees. It is used for decoration at Christmas.

mistrust not to trust or not to believe someone

misunderstand not to understand; to mistake the meaning of something

mite anything very small. In the old days there was a very small coin called a mite. The same word also means a kind of tiny insect.

mittens coverings for the hands, like gloves, but without places for the fingers

mix to put different things together

mixture two or more things put together

moan a long low sound made by someone in pain or sorrow

moat a big ditch, usually filled with water. In olden times, castles had deep moats around them so that enemies could not get across.

mock to make fun of someone

model a copy of something like a boat or airplane, usually smaller than the real thing. The same word also means someone who shows off clothes or someone who stays quite still so that artists can paint or draw pictures of them.

moderate   fair; between bad and good

modern   nowadays; at this time, not old-fashioned

moist   damp; slightly wet

moisture   dampness; slight wetness

mold   a container into which you pour liquid that will get hard, and will have the shape of the container when you turn it out. The same word also means a green or gray furry covering that grows on stale bread or cheese.

mole   a small animal with sharp claws, tiny eyes and dark thick fur. It digs long tunnels in the ground. The same word also means a small, dark spot on the skin.

moment   a very short time

monarch   a king, queen, emperor or empress

monastery   a building where monks live

money   coins and paper banknotes

mongrel   a dog which is a mixture of different types

monitor   a pupil in a school who is given a special job to help the teacher

monk   a member of a religious group living in a monastery

monkey   a small lively animal with a long tail. Monkeys live in hot countries, and are very good at climbing trees and swinging from branch to branch.

monster   an enormous, horrible creature; a plant or
 animal of unusual or frightening appearance

month   about 4 weeks. There are 12 months in a
 year.

monument   a statue or building that is put up to
 make people remember someone or some
 event

mood   how you feel in your mind. You can be in a
 good mood when you are happy, or in a bad
 mood when something has made you cross or
 unhappy.

moon   the largest and brightest light we can see in
 the sky at night. It revolves round the earth.

mop   pieces of sponge or thick cotton fastened on a
 long stick, used to clean floors or wash dishes

morning   the time between dawn and midday

mortar   a mixture of cement, sand and water used
 in building to make bricks stick together

mosaic   a pattern or picture made by arranging lots
 of small pieces of colored glass or stones

mosquito   a small flying insect that bites

moss   a very small green plant that looks like velvet.
 It grows close to the ground in damp places,
 especially in the woods.

moth   an insect rather like a butterfly, except that it
 only flies at night. The grubs of some small
 moths eat holes in your clothes.

mother   a woman who has a family

motor   a machine which makes something work or
 move

motorbike   a kind of heavy bicycle with a motor

motto   a short saying which gives a rule for behavior, such as *Be prepared*

mound   a heap of stones or earth; a small rounded hill

mount   another word for mountain. The same word also means to get up on something, like a horse or a bicycle.

mountain   a very high hill

mouse   a little animal with a long tail and sharp teeth

moustache (*say mustash*)   the hair that grows above a man's upper lip

mouth   the opening in your face which you use for speaking and eating

move   to go, or make something go, from one place to another

movement   the act of moving

movie theater   a building where films are shown

mow (*rhymes with go*)   to cut grass or hay

much   a lot

muck   damp dirt or rubbish; manure

mud   soft wet earth

muddle   to make a mess of things; to do things in a confused way

muff   a tube-shaped piece of fur or warm material. You put your hands in through the openings to keep them warm.

muffin   a soft cake-like bread, eaten with butter

muffler   a woolly scarf

mug   a large heavy cup with straight sides

mulberry   a tree with berries something like raspberries. Mulberry leaves are the main food of silkworms.

mule   an animal whose parents are a donkey and a horse

multiply   to increase or make something a number of times larger

mumble   to speak with your mouth nearly closed so that your words are not heard clearly

mumps   a very uncomfortable illness. You have a fever, your neck swells up, and it hurts to swallow.

munch   to chew with a crunching sound

municipal   having to do with a city

murder   to kill someone against the law of a country, not by accident or in wartime

murderer   someone who kills another person against the law

murmur   a gentle soft sound that goes on and on

muscle   the fleshy parts of the body that tighten and loosen to make it move

museum   a place where interesting collections of things are set out for people to look at

mushroom   a small plant shaped like an umbrella. It can be cooked and eaten.

music   pleasing sounds that you sing or play on a musical instrument

must   to have to do something, such as going to school every day

mustard   a kind of brown-yellow paste, sometimes eaten with meat. It has a very strong flavor and makes your tongue feel hot.

mutiny   a refusal by soldiers, sailors or airmen to obey their officers

mutter   to speak so softly that it is hard to understand the words

mutton   the meat from sheep

muzzle   the jaws and nose of an animal. The same word also means a sort of cage or arrangement of straps fastened on an animal's nose and mouth to keep it from biting.

myself   me and no one else

mystery   something strange that has happened, but that cannot be explained or easily understood

myth   an old, old story which explains how something began or happened. The same word also means an imaginary person or event.

nag   to keep on scolding or finding fault

nail   the hard part at the end of a finger or toe. The same word also means a thin sharp piece of metal used to join pieces of wood.

naked   without clothes or covering

name   what a person or thing is called

nanny-goat   a female goat

nap   a short sleep

napkin   a square piece of cloth or paper used to wipe your mouth and fingers when you are eating

narcissus   a spring flower, white or yellow, that smells very sweet

narrow   slim; thin; not wide

nasturtium   a plant with lots of round leaves and orange, red and yellow colored flowers

nasty   not nice; not pleasant

nation   all the people living in one country under one government

national   belonging to one nation or country

native   a person born in a particular place or country

natural   not man-made

nature   everything in the world that is not man-made

naughty   not doing what you should; behaving badly

navigate   to steer or guide a ship or airplane

navy   a nation's warships and the sailors who run them

near close to; not far away

nearly very closely; almost; not far from

neat tidy; in good order

necessary having to be done; needed

neck the part of your body between your head and your shoulders

necklace a string of beads or thin chain worn round the neck

nectar a sweet juice found in some flower blossoms

need to have to have something. You need clothes to keep you warm.

needle a long, thin pointed piece of metal used for sewing. There are also special needles for knitting.

negative meaning or saying *no*

neglect to forget or be careless about looking after something

neigh the cry a horse makes, usually when it is frightened or excited

neighbor a person who lives near you

neither not one or the other

nephew the son of a brother or sister

nerve one of the small thread-like parts of your body that carries messages to and from the brain so that you can move and feel. The same word also means courage and daring.

nervous jumpy; easily frightened

nest a bird's home, where the eggs are laid and hatched out

net pieces of string knotted together so that there are more holes than string

nettle a weed with prickly hairs that sting if they touch your skin

never not ever; not at any time

new only just made; not old; not seen before

newborn just born

news things that have just happened

newspaper a printed daily or weekly paper that tells you about things that have just happened

newt a small animal like a lizard that can live on land as well as in water

next the nearest; the one after

nib the metal point of a pen

nibble to eat with tiny bites

nice kind; friendly; pretty; pleasant

nick a little cut in something

nickel a silvery-gray metal

nickname a name you give to someone for fun, to describe what he is like, such as *shorty* for someone who is not very tall

niece   the daughter of a brother or sister

night   the time between sunset and sunrise, when the sky is dark

nightdress   a garment worn in bed by girls and women

nightgown   another word for nightdress

nightingale   a small brown bird whose song is even more beautiful at night than in the daytime

nimble   quick or clever in moving or climbing

nip   to pinch or bite off a little bit of something

no   the opposite of *yes*. The same word also means not any.

noble   great; grand

nobleman   a man of high rank

nobody   no one; no person

nod   to bend your head forward and back to show you agree. The same word also means to let your head fall forward when you are sleepy.

noise   a sound, sometimes very loud

nomad   one of a group of people who have no permanent home, but who roam about looking for food for themselves and their animals

none   not one; not any

nonsense   talk which means nothing

noon   12 o'clock in the day; midday

noose a loop in a rope, with a slip-knot that can be tightened by pulling it

normal ordinary; usual

north the direction which is the opposite of south, on your left as you face the rising sun

nose the part of your face with which you smell, and through which you breathe

nosey wanting to know all about other people's belongings and activities

nostril one of the two openings in your nose

note a short letter. The same word also means a sound in music or a piece of paper money.

notebook a little book in which you write things down that you don't want to forget

nothing not anything

notice to see something. The same word also means a printed piece of paper announcing something.

nought nothing

nourish to feed

novel new and different. The same word also means a long story about imaginary people.

novelty something new and different

now at this time

nowhere not anywhere or any place

nozzle a spout at the end of a pipe or hose

nude naked; without clothing

nudge to poke or push someone gently with your elbow

nuisance something or someone who gets in the way of what others want to do

numb not able to feel, as when your fingers are numb with cold

number a word which says how many. One (1), two (2), three (3), and four (4) are numbers.

numeral a figure; a number such as 1, 2 or 3

numerous very many

nun a female member of a religious group living in a convent

nurse someone who helps the doctor to look after people who are ill

nursery a room or building where very young children sleep or play

nut a fruit or seed with a hard shell. The same word also means a piece of metal with a hole through it that you screw on to the end of a bolt.

nutmeg a hard spicy seed used to flavor food

nylon a man-made material used for making clothing, brushes and other useful things

oak a kind of tree that can grow very big and lives to a very old age. It has acorns as its fruit.

oar a long piece of wood with one flat end, used to row a boat

oasis a place in a desert where plants and trees grow because there is water

oath a solemn promise that you will speak the truth or keep your word

oats a kind of grain used mostly to feed animals. Oats are also ground up and cooked with water to make porridge.

obedience doing as you are told

obey to do as you are told

object a thing; something you can see or handle. The same word also means to disagree with someone else's idea.

oblige to force someone to do something. The same word also means to do someone a favor.

oblong a squared shape with four straight sides. Two opposite sides are of equal length and the other sides are also equal but longer or shorter than the first two.

observe to watch carefully; to notice

obstacle anything that stands in the way so that you cannot go forward

obstinate wanting your own way; stubborn

obtain another word for get

occasion a particular event or happening

occupation the kind of work that you do

occupy to live in, as when a family occupies a house. The same word also means to go into enemy land in wartime and take over towns and cities.

occur to happen

ocean a very big sea

o'clock   the time by the clock

octopus   a sea creature with eight arms covered with
    suckers

odd   strange; queer. The same word also means not
    even in number (1, 3, 5, 7, 9 are odd numbers).

odor   smell

offend   to do something wrong; to displease; to
    make someone angry

offense   a crime. The same word also means
    something that hurts someone's feelings or
    makes him angry.

offensive   causing hurt; unpleasant

offer   to say you will do or give something

office   a building or room where people work
    with business papers

officer   someone who commands others, as in the
    army, navy or air force

often   many times; happening over and over again

oil   a thick greasy liquid which can come from
    animals or plants, or from under the ground

ointment   a soothing paste you put on sores or cuts

O.K.   all right

old   having been alive or on earth for a long time

olden   long ago, as when we say in olden days or in
    olden times

older having lived longer than someone else, or existed longer than something else

old-fashioned of times long ago; not modern

omelet eggs beaten up, fried until the mixture is almost solid, and then folded over

omit to leave out; not to do something

once for one time only; at a time long ago

onion a bulb-like vegetable with a strong smell and flavor

only single; one and no more

open not shut; able to let things through

opening an open place; a hole or space

operation something that is done, especially something done by doctors in a hospital to make people well again

opinion what you think about something

opportunity a chance to do something

opposite as different as possible from something else; across from

optical having to do with eyes or with seeing

orange a sweet fruit. The same word also means the color of the fruit.

orangutan a large reddish-brown ape that lives in jungles

orbit the path in which something moves around another thing in space

orchard a lot of fruit trees growing together

order a command. The same word also means to ask for something to be done, such as for something to be sent to you from a shop.

ordinary usual; not special or different

ore rock or mineral from which we get metal

organ a large musical instrument with a keyboard and pipes that the sounds come from

organization a group of people or of nations who get together to work for a particular purpose; such as the World Health Organization

organize to get a group of people together for a particular purpose: to plan and arrange something

ornament anything used to make something look prettier, such as jewelry or a vase

orphan a child whose mother and father are both dead

ostrich a very large bird which has long legs but which cannot fly because its wings are too small

otherwise if not; if things are different

otter a furry web-footed swimming animal rather like a large weasel

ought   must; should

ounce   a measurement of weight. There are 16 ounces in a pound.

outburst   a sudden bursting out, such as cheering when a goal is scored at a football game

outfit   a set of clothing or equipment

outing   a pleasure trip or walk

outlaw   a person who fights against the law and is told that he cannot be protected by the law. Robin Hood and his men were outlaws.

outline   a line drawn to show the shape of something round the outside edge. The same word also means the main ideas of a story or a plan.

outside   the opposite of inside; out of doors

oval   egg-shaped. A football is oval.

oven   the inside part of a stove where you bake things

overcoat   an outdoor coat worn over all your other clothes

overcome   to get the better of someone or something; to defeat

overflow   to spill over the top of a container because it is too full

overhang   to hang out over; to stick out over

overtake   to catch up with and go in front of someone or something

overthrow   to destroy or defeat completely

owe to need to pay for something you have bought

owl a bird with big eyes and a sharp curved beak. Owls fly at night and sleep through the day.

own to have something that belongs to you

oyster a shellfish with a very hard flat shell in two parts

oxen bulls and cows

pace a step or the length of a step, as when you say something is six paces away

pack to put things into a container. You pack clothes into a trunk or suitcase when you go away. The same word also means a bundle of things carried on your back.

package a parcel or bundle

packet a small parcel or package

pad a lot of sheets of paper glued or sewn together at the top. The same word also means a piece of thick, soft material, usually to protect a part of your body from harm.

paddle a pole with a broad part at the end, which you use to move a canoe through the water. The same word also means to walk around in water up to your ankles.

page one side of a sheet of paper in a book, newspaper, magazine or notebook. The same word also means a young boy who attends a bride at her wedding, or who runs errands in a hotel.

pageant a show in costume, usually about things that happened long ago

pail another word for bucket

pain   the feeling when something hurts you

paint   to color something with a brush and colored liquid called paint

painting   a colored picture painted on paper or canvas

pair   two things which are meant to be used together, like a pair of shoes

pajamas   a sleeping suit

palace   the house where a king or queen lives

pale   not having much color or brightness; looking washed out

paling   one of the pieces of wood in a special kind of fence

palm   the inside of your hand between your fingers and your wrist. The same word also means a tall tree with large fan-shaped leaves at the top. It grows in hot countries.

pan   a metal container with a handle, used for cooking

pancake   a thin round cake eaten hot. You cook it in a frying pan.

panda   a large black and white wild animal, something like a bear. Some pandas are much smaller and look rather like a large cat with a bushy tail and a pointed nose.

panic   sudden fear or terror that keeps people from thinking reasonably

pansy a small garden plant with velvety, brightly colored flowers

pant to gasp for breath

panther a kind of leopard

pantomime a play in which the actors do not speak

pantry a small room or cupboard where food is kept

pants trousers

paper the material used to write on or wrap parcels in

parable a fable or story that is meant to show you how to behave towards others

parachute a large piece of strong cloth which is fastened to a man who is going to jump from an airplane. It opens like an umbrella, and brings him safely and slowly to the ground.

parade a lot of people walking or marching together, sometimes in costume

paraffin a colorless wax found in the earth or made from coal, wood or petroleum

parallel going in the same direction the same distance apart and never meeting, like a pair of railroad lines

parcel a bundle of things, usually tied up in paper

parchment   the skin of a goat, sheep or other animal, cleaned and dried. In olden days, before paper was invented, it was used to write on.

pardon   to forgive

parent   a mother or a father

parish   a part of a county with its own church

park   an open space with grass and trees and playgrounds for children. The same word also means to stop a car and leave it at the side of the street or in a parking space.

parlor   another word for living-room

parrot   a brightly-colored bird often kept as a pet in a cage. Some parrots can imitate talking.

parsnip   a vegetable with a thick whitish root shaped rather like a carrot

part   a piece of something. The same word also means to leave someone.

particle   a tiny bit or piece of something

particular   single or special. The same word also means fussy or very careful.

partner   a person who shares equally, or who plays or works with another person

partridge   a plump wild bird rather like a small pheasant

party   a lot of people all together having a good time

pass   to move ahead of something in front of you. The same word also means to hand something to someone.

passage   a long narrow part inside a building, with doors opening at the sides and end of it

passenger   someone who rides in a vehicle but who is not the driver

passport   special papers from the government that help you to travel in other countries

paste   a thick white liquid, used to stick paper and other things together

pastime   a game or hobby that you like to do to pass the time

pastry   a mixture of flour and water and fat which is rolled flat before it is baked

pasture   a field where sheep and cattle are allowed to eat the grass

pat   to hit something very lightly

patch   a small piece of cloth used to cover a hole in clothes. The same word also means a small piece of ground.

pate   the top of the head

patent   a government paper that keeps other people from using an invention without permission

path   a narrow way along which people may travel, usually on foot

patience   the ability to wait for something without making a fuss

patient   able to wait for something without making a fuss; taking a lot of trouble to get something right. The same word also means a sick person who is being looked after by a doctor.

patter   to tap lightly and quickly. Rain patters on the roof.

pattern   curved or straight lines repeated many times over, as on a patterned carpet or wallpaper. The same word also means a model or plan to help you make something, like a dress pattern.

pause   to stop what you are doing for a moment

pavement   a hard path at the side of the street for people to walk safely

paw   the foot of a four-legged animal which has claws

pay   to give money for something you have bought or for work someone has done

pea   one of the round green seeds which are used as food. Peas grow in pods on a climbing plant.

peace   a time when no one is fighting

peach   a juicy round fruit with a velvety skin and a stone-like seed

peacock   a large bird with beautifully-colored feathers. He can spread his tail out like a large fan.

peak   the topmost point. The same word also means the brim of a cap that sticks out in front.

peal   a loud sound, as of bells ringing, or of thunder

peanut   a nut which grows underground in a pod

pear   a juicy fruit rather like an apple, only softer
and cone-shaped

pearl   a small creamy-white jewel, used for
necklaces and other jewelry. Pearls grow
inside some oyster shells.

pebble   a small smooth roundish piece of stone

peck   to pick up food in the beak with short jerky
movements. Hens peck at their food.

peculiar   odd; strange; unusual

pedal   a foot lever to make something work.
Bicycles have pedals and so have
pianos.

pedestrian   someone who is walking

peel   the skin of fruit or vegetables. You can
peel bark off trees and sometimes pieces of
your skin when you have been
sunburned.

peep   to take a quick look

peer   to look very closely

peg   a strong clip or pin used to hang things up—
like washing on a line, or to fasten things down
—like a tent rope

pekinese   a small, fluffy dog with almost no nose

pelican a big water-bird which has a large pouch under the lower part of its beak. It can scoop up fish in its pouch, and store them there until it wants to eat.

pellet a tiny ball of something, such as paper, clay or metal

pelt the skin or hide of an animal. The same word also means to throw something, such as snowballs, or to pour down, like heavy rain.

pen a tool used for writing with ink

penalty a punishment for breaking a rule

pencil a thin tool for writing and drawing. It is made of wood with a stick of black or colored material in the middle.

pendulum a weight on the end of a rod that swings from side to side as in a clock

penguin a web-footed swimming bird that lives near the South Pole. It has short legs and wings but cannot fly.

penknife a small knife that you can carry in your pocket

penny a piece of money

people men, women, boys and girls

pepper a spicy powder used to flavor food. It tastes hot, and can make you sneeze if you breathe it in. The same word also means a bright green or red vegetable that grows in hot countries.

peppermint a green plant used for flavoring sauces, drinks and sweets

perch something a bird sits or stands on, like a stick or twig

percussion all those musical instruments, such as a drum or cymbals, that are banged or struck

perfect without any faults or mistakes

perform to do or act: to play a part on the stage or to play a musical instrument

performance an act: a play or other entertainment

perfume a sweet smell; a liquid having a sweet smell

perhaps possibly; maybe

peril great danger

perimeter the outside measurement of a figure or area

period a length of time

periscope a tube containing mirrors used in submarines or underground so that people can see what is going on above them

perish to die or be destroyed

permanent long-lasting, not ever changing

permission freedom given to do something, as when you are given permission to stay up especially late to watch television

permit to allow; to give permission

persist to keep on trying to do something or asking for something

person a man, woman or child

personal belonging to one person

perspire to give off sweat from your skin when you are very hot

persuade to talk someone into doing something, even if he doesn't want to

pest something or someone that makes difficulties for others; a nuisance

pet an animal that is kept at home; not wild. Dogs and cats are pets.

petal the part of a flower that grows out from the middle

petrel a small seabird with long wings

petroleum oil obtained from wells drilled in the ground

petticoat a skirt worn under dresses by girls and women

petty small; unimportant

pew a long wooden bench with a back, for people to sit on in church

pheasant a bird, usually wild, with beautiful long tail feathers

phonograph an instrument on which you can play records of music or words

photograph a picture taken with a camera

phrase a group of words, usually part of a sentence

physical to do with nature or with the body.
Physical Education exercises your
muscles.

piano a large musical instrument with a keyboard

pick to choose; to gather. The same word also
means a sharp tool used to break rock or hard
ground.

pickle to keep in vinegar cooked vegetables like
beets and cucumbers

picnic an outing when you take food to eat out of
doors

picture a drawing, painting or photograph

pie food made of pastry outside, and filled with
fruit or meat

piece a part or bit of something, but not all of it,
like a piece of pie. The word also means one of
something, like a piece of paper.

pier a platform of stone, wood or metal, that
reaches out over the water so that ships and
boats can stop at the end of it

pierce to make a hole with something sharp

pig a fat farm animal with a curly tail

pigeon a plump bird with short legs, that makes a
cooing sound. Some pigeons are kept as pets
and some are used to carry messages or for
racing.

pigmy one of a tribe of very small people who live in the jungles of some hot countries. The word can also be spelled pygmy.

pigsty a place where pigs are kept

pigtail a braid or plait of hair hanging from the back of the head

pike a large greedy freshwater fish. The same word also means a weapon like a spear, used in the old days.

pile a lot of things on top of each other, like a pile of books, or a pile of old junk

pilgrim someone who travels a long way to visit a holy place

pill medicine like a little ball or pellet, that must be swallowed

pillar a large post of stone or wood, used to hold up part of a building

pillow a bag filled with feathers or some soft material, where you lay your head in bed

pillowcase a covering for a pillow. The word pillowslip has the same meaning.

pilot a man who steers a ship into harbor or who controls an airplane

pimple a small pointed swelling on the skin

pin a thin pointed piece of metal used for fastening or holding things together

pinafore a sleeveless garment worn as an apron or sometimes as a dress

pincers a small tool used for holding things steady or pulling nails out of wood

pinch to squeeze something tightly, usually between finger and thumb

pine an evergreen tree with cones and leaves like needles

pineapple a sweet-tasting fruit that looks something like a large pine cone. It grows in hot countries.

pink a very pale red color. The same word also means a garden flower with a sweet spicy smell.

pint a measure for liquid

pip a fruit seed

pipe any tube, usually of metal, through which a liquid (such as water) or gas flows. The same word also means a small bowl on the end of a tube, used for smoking tobacco.

pirate someone who robs ships at sea

pistol a small hand gun that can be carried in the pocket

pit a hole in the ground. The same word also means the hard stone in some fruits.

pitch to throw or fall forward: to set something up, such as a tent or a stall in a market. The same word also means the highness or lowness of musical notes.

pitcher a person who throws a ball in some games. The same word also means a large jug for holding or pouring liquids.

pitchfork a tool used for lifting hay

pity a feeling of sadness you have because someone else is ill or unhappy

pivot the pin or center on which something turns

pixie a kind of fairy

placard a written or printed poster or notice

place somewhere where something is

plague a terrible illness that spreads from person to person very quickly

plaid (*rhymes with sad*) a piece of woolen cloth with a checked or tartan pattern

plain ordinary; not fancy or decorated. The same word also means a large flat part of the country.

plait (*rhymes with mat*) several pieces of ribbon, straw or hair twisted under and over each other, like a rope

plan to think out how a thing can be done before you do it. The same word also means a model or drawing showing the shape and design of something, like a building or a town.

plane a carpenter's tool used to make wood smooth. It is also a short word for airplane.

planet anything in the sky which, like the earth, goes round the sun

plank   a long flat heavy piece of wood, thicker than a board

plant   anything that grows up from the earth, like grass or flowers

plaster   a mixture of water, sand and lime, which hardens when it is put on walls and ceilings. The same word also means a piece of sticky tape that holds a bandage in place.

plastic   material that can be molded into different shapes when it is soft. Later it becomes hard. Lots of things are made of plastic, such as combs, cups and buckets.

plate   a round flat dish for food

platform   the raised part of a hall or theater for the speakers or actors. The same word also means the part of a railway station beside the tracks, where you get on to a train.

play   to have fun: to take part in a game: to perform on a musical instrument. The same word also means a show acted on a stage, usually without music.

playground   a special place at school or in a park where children can play

playmate   someone you play with

playtime   a period of time for playing, not working or studying

pleasant   nice; agreeable; enjoyable

please   to make someone feel happy. You also use this word when you are being polite in asking someone to do something.

pleasure a feeling of being glad and happy when you are enjoying yourself

pleat a fold in cloth, pressed or stitched down to keep it in place

plenty more than enough; all that is needed

pliers a tool, like small pincers, used to twist or bend wire

plod to walk heavily and slowly

plot a small piece of land. The same word also means the main happenings in a play or story. Sometimes it means a wicked or evil plan.

plow a farm tool pulled along by horses or a tractor. It cuts into the ground and turns it over.

pluck courage; bravery. The same word also means to pull at the strings of a musical instrument, such as the guitar.

plug a piece of metal or rubber made to fit a hole so the water doesn't run out. An electric plug fits into a socket to obtain electric power.

plum a juicy fruit with a pit in the middle

plumber a man who connects up or mends water pipes

plume a large curly feather, sometimes worn as an ornament on a hat

plump rather fat and well-rounded

plunge to throw yourself into water; to rush into something

plural   more than one. The plural of cat is cats.

plus   the sign + which shows that numbers are to be added

plywood   very thin layers of wood glued together

pneumonia (*say newmonia*)   a painful illness of the lungs

poach   to cook foods, such as eggs without their shells, or fish, in very hot water. The same word also means to catch animals or fish on someone else's land without his permission.

pocket   a little bag sewn into clothes to put things in

pod   the outside covering of seeds

poem   a piece of writing, like a song without music, that shows your thoughts and imaginings

poet   someone who writes poems

poetry   the art of writing poetry. The same word also means poems as in *a book of poetry*.

point   the sharp end of something, like a pin or a pencil

pointed   sharp; with a point; like the end of a pin

poison   something swallowed or injected that can make you very ill or even kill you

poke   to jab or push anything suddenly

poker   a metal rod used for stirring a fire. The same word is the name of a card game.

polar   having to do with the North and South Poles. Polar bears live near the North Pole.

pole   a long rounded piece of wood or metal, used

to hold something up, such as a flag. The same word also means the north or south ends of the world's axis.

police   a group of men and women whose job is to see that the laws of the country are obeyed. If you see someone breaking the law, you can ask the police to do something about it.

polish   to make something shiny by rubbing it hard, usually with special powder, paste or liquid

polite   having good manners

pollen   yellow powder in the middle of flowers

poncho   an outer garment like a blanket with a hole in the middle for the head to go through

pond   a small lake

pony   a little horse

poodle   a kind of dog with very curly hair

pool   a small area of water, sometimes no bigger than a puddle

poor   having little money or few belongings. The same word also means not good, like poor soil where nothing grows very well.

pop   a sharp quick exploding sound. The same word can be short for popular. Then it means music or art that most people like.

popcorn   a special kind of corn that makes a popping sound and bursts open when it is heated

poplar   a tall, straight, narrow tree

poppy   a plant, usually with bright red flowers, often seen growing wild in the fields in summer

popular   liked by most people

population   the people, or the number of people living in any country, city, town or village

porch   a covered entrance to a building

porcupine   a wild animal with a coat of quills mixed with hairs

pork   pigmeat

porpoise   a sea animal, rather like a small whale with a blunt snout

porridge   a cooked breakfast food made from ground-up oats

port   a harbor, or a town with a harbor

porter   a man who carries your luggage. The same word also means someone who lets people in or out of a door or a gate at the entrance to a building.

portion   a part; a helping of food

portrait   a painting or drawing of a person

positive   meaning *yes*: absolutely sure

possible   able to be done

post   a long piece of wood or metal, fastened in the ground so that it stands up straight. The same word also means letters and parcels sent and delivered; another word for mail.

postcard a piece of thin cardboard on which you can write to your friends. Most postcards have a picture on the back.

poster a large notice or picture that tells you about something that is going to happen. Some posters show you pictures of things you can buy, like food or clothes.

postman a man who collects and delivers the mail

post office the place where you buy stamps and licenses. It is also the place where all letters and parcels are sorted before they are delivered.

postpone to put off to another time

posy a small bunch of flowers

pot any deep dish for cooking. The same word also means plastic or clay containers for plants.

potato a vegetable that grows under the ground

potter someone who makes pots and other things out of clay

pottery crockery, ornaments and other things made out of baked clay

pouch a small bag

pounce to spring or jump down on something suddenly

pound a measure of weight. The same word also means to hit something with very heavy blows, like pounding on a locked door.

pour   to make liquid run out of a container by tipping it forward

pout   to close your lips and push them out to show that you are not pleased

powder   very tiny dustlike bits of something. Flour and cocoa are powders.

power   ability to do something; strength

practical   useful

practice   something done over and over until you are good at it, like throwing a ball, or playing a musical instrument

prairie   a large area of flat grassy land with very few trees

praise   to say very nice things about someone or something

pray   to ask God for help; to request humbly

prayer   the act of praying

preach   to speak to others about being good, usually in church

precious   very valuable; worth a lot of money

precipice   a steep cliff

preface   a short beginning to a book to explain what it is about

prefer   to like one thing better than another

prefix a syllable at the beginning of a word which changes its meaning. If you put *un* before the word *pleasant* it changes the meaning to *not pleasant*.

pregnant carrying a baby or babies not yet born

prepare to make or get something ready

present something that is given to you. The same word also means at this time; now.

president the chief person in the government of a country that hasn't a king or queen. The same word can also mean the most important man in a club or business.

press to push against or push down. The same word also means all newspapers and magazines and the people who write what is printed in them.

pressure force or weight pushing against something

pretend to make believe

pretty lovely; beautiful

prevent to stop something from happening

previous happening or occurring before some other event

prey a bird or animal that is hunted for food by another bird or animal

price how much money you have to pay for something

prick to make a tiny hole with something sharp. You must be careful not to prick your finger with a needle when you are sewing.

prickle a sharp point growing on the stem of a plant or on an animal. The thorns on a rosebush are prickles, and so are the stiff hairs on a hedgehog.

pride a high opinion of how clever you are and how nice you look. Sometimes it means a feeling of pleasure about something you have done well.

priest a man in charge of a church who leads the prayers there

primary first of all

primer a first book for teaching children to read

prince the son of a king or queen

princess the daughter of a king or queen

principal a man or woman who is responsible for all the teachers and pupils in a school

print to press words and pictures on paper with a heavy machine

prison a place where people who do things against the law have to stay for a period of time

prisoner someone who has been captured in war or who is locked up in a prison because he has done something wrong

private belonging to one person or group of people. The same word also means a soldier in the army.

prize a reward for doing something well

probable likely to happen

problem   a question that is difficult to answer or decide

proceed   to go ahead; to go on

procession   a large number of people or vehicles moving along in a line

prod   to poke

produce   to make; to cause; to bring into being

producer   someone who produces something, especially a film or play

profession   a kind of work that needs special study and training, such as the nursing profession or the teaching profession

profit   gain; the money left over after you have paid all your expenses

program   a printed paper giving information about a performance

progress   movement forward or onward; improvement

prohibit   to forbid or prevent

promenade   a public footpath in a park or at the seaside where you walk for pleasure

promise   to say that you will or will not do something, without fail

prompt   quick; at once; with no delay

prong   one of the sharp spikes on a fork

pronounce   to speak or sound out words

proof   a way of showing that what is said is true

prop   a long piece of wood or metal that is put under something to keep it from falling down

propel   to drive forward

propeller   the part of a ship or airplane that drives it forward

proper   right; as it should be

properly   in the right way

property   something that belongs to someone

prophecy   what someone says will happen in the future

prophesy   to say what will happen in the future

propose   to suggest something, such as a plan of action or way of going about things

prosecute   to speak against someone in a court of law because he is supposed to have done something wrong

protect   to guard or defend

protest   to object to something; to disagree

proud   having a feeling of pride; pleased that you are good at something

prove   to show that what is said is true

proverb   a well-known short saying which is often used to show you how you should act, like *Least said soonest mended*

provide   to supply; to give what is needed

prowl   to move about silently and secretly

pry   to peer into or try to find out about things that do not concern you

public   open to or belonging to everyone; the opposite of private

pudding   a soft, sweet food eaten at the end of a meal. Puddings are usually made with flour or grain, eggs, milk and sugar.

puddle   a small pool of water, usually left in the road after it has been raining

puff   to blow air or smoke out of the mouth. The same word also means a soft piece of material used to put powder on the skin.

puffin   a sea bird with a short thick beak

pull   to get hold of something and bring it towards you

pulley   a wheel with a hollow rim. You put a rope around the rim and pull on it to lift heavy things.

pullover   a knitted garment with sleeves

pump   a machine used to get water from a well. The same word also means the machine you use to put air into tires.

pumpkin   a large yellow- or orange-colored fruit that grows on a vine on the ground

punch   to hit hard, usually with your fists

punctual   on time; not late

punctuate   to divide writing into phrases or sentences by using special marks, such as a period (.), question mark (?) or comma (,)

puncture   to make a hole in something

punish   to make someone suffer or pay for doing something wrong

punishment   something that makes a person suffer or pay for wrong-doing

punt   a kick in football when the ball is dropped from the hands and kicked before it touches the ground.

pupil   a person who is taught by a teacher. The same word also means the round dark circle in the middle of your eye through which you see.

puppet   a doll which can be moved by pulling strings or putting your hand inside it

puppy   a young dog

purchase   to buy something

pure   clean; without fault

purl   a knitting stitch, the opposite to plain stitch

purple   a color made by mixing red and blue

purpose   something you plan to do

purr   the sound a cat makes when it is happy

purse   a small bag to keep money in

pursue to go after, to follow

push to move something away from you without lifting it

put to place something

puzzle a kind of game or question. You have to think very hard to get the answer.

pygmy one of a tribe of very small people who live in the jungles of some hot countries. The word can also be spelled pigmy.

pylon a metal tower or mast that holds up electric cables

pyramid a solid shape with flat triangular sides, usually on a square base

python a large dangerous snake that can kill people by squeezing them in its coils

quack the noise a duck makes

quail a wild bird like a small partridge. The same word also means to lose courage.

quaint old-fashioned; a little odd

quake to tremble, shake or quiver

quality how good or bad something is. Clothes of good quality usually cost more but will last longer than clothes of poor quality.

quantity   the size, number or amount of things

quarrel   to argue or disagree with someone in an angry way

quarry   a place where stone for building is dug out. The same word also means an animal that is being hunted.

quart   a measure of liquid equal to two pints

quarter   one-fourth of anything, a fourth part

quay (*say kee*)   a landing place for boats or ships

queen   a woman who is the ruler of a country, or the wife of a king

queer   odd; strange; not ordinary

quench   to put an end to something, as when you quench your thirst by having a drink, or when you quench a fire by putting water on it

query   a question

question   something someone wants to know

queue (*say kew*)   a line of people waiting their turn. The same word also means a pigtail at the back of the head.

quick   fast; in a very short time

quiet   not making a noise; silent; at rest

quill   the hard stiff part of a feather: one of the sharp spines on some animals, such as porcupines

quilt   a thick padded bedcover

quit   to leave; to go away

quiver to tremble or shiver. The same word also means a case for arrows.

quiz a lot of questions to find out how much someone knows

rabbit a small furry animal with long ears. Some rabbits are kept in hutches as pets, but wild rabbits dig holes in the ground to live in.

raccoon a North American tree-dwelling animal with a bushy, striped tail. It is most active at night.

race to move very quickly to get to a place before someone else does. The same word also means a large group of people having a similar appearance, especially the same skin color. Europeans, Africans and Chinese all belong to different races.

racetrack the path or course where a race is run

rack a framework to keep things on, such as a hat rack

racket a bat with a network of strings used in playing tennis and other games. Sometimes the word is spelled racquet. The same word also means a loud noise.

radiant bright; sending out rays of heat or light. The same word also means showing joy.

radiate to send out rays of heat or light: to spread out in many directions from a center

radiator a set of pipes or other apparatus used to heat a room by electricity, hot water or steam. The same word also means the part of a car that holds water to keep the engine from getting too hot.

radio   an instrument that brings broadcast music and other people's voices through the air from far away

radish   the small red and white root of a plant, used in salads

radius   a straight line from the center of a circle to its outer edge

raffia   strips of palm leaves used to make things such as mats and baskets

raft   floating logs or boards fastened together

rag   a piece of cloth that is old and often full of holes

rage   great anger; fury

raid   a quick surprise attack

rail   a wooden or metal bar used as part of a fence: a long metal bar which is used to make a railroad track

railing   a fence of posts and rails

railroad   very long parallel bars of metal that make a road or track for trains to run on

rain   drops of water that fall out of the clouds

rainbow   a beautifully-colored arch that you can see in the sky when the sun shines through rain

raincoat   a coat made of rubber or some other material that doesn't let the rain through

rainfall   the amount of rain that falls in a certain period of time

raise   to lift up. The same word means to collect,

as when you raise money for charity. It also means to grow or breed something, like plants or animals.

raisin a dried grape used in cakes and puddings

rake a garden tool with a long handle and metal teeth

ram a male sheep. The same word also means to push hard or crash into something.

ramble to stroll about for pleasure. The same word also means a long walk in the country.

ranch a very big farm where large numbers of cattle, horses or sheep are raised

ranger a man who is paid to look after a forest or large area of land

rank the position of a soldier, sailor or airman in the armed forces. The same word also means a row or line of things or people.

ransack to search through something in a rather rough and untidy way

ransom a sum of money paid for the safe return of someone who has been captured or kidnapped

rap to hit sharply

rapid quick; speedy

rapids a rocky, steep part of a river where the water flows very quickly

rapier a long thin sword

rare unusual; valuable

rascal a dishonest person; one who makes mischief or who cannot be trusted

rash   an outbreak of red spots on the skin. The same word also means acting hastily, without careful thought.

raspberry   a small soft red fruit with lots of seeds

rat   an animal like a large mouse, with long sharp teeth

rate   how fast something happens. The same word also means how much you pay for something.

rather   somewhat; to some extent

ration   a share or portion. When there is not enough food to go round, everyone is allowed the same ration, so that everyone has a fair share.

rattle   the noise you hear when you shake hard things together

rattlesnake   a poisonous snake with rattling bony rings on its tail

raw   not cooked

ray   a thin line of light, like a sunbeam

rayon   a man-made silky material. Dresses, blouses, ties and other clothes are often made of rayon.

razor   a very sharp instrument, used to shave hair off

reach   to stretch out far enough to touch or get hold of something. The same word also means to get to a place; to arrive.

read   to understand printed or written words

ready   able to do something at once; prepared

real   true; not made up or imaginary

realize   to understand clearly

really   without question; in fact

reap   to cut and gather in crops of grain

rear   the back part

reason   why something is done or said; an explanation

reasonable   sensible; fair; good enough

rebel   to go against someone in authority

receipt   a written or printed note that proves you have paid for something

receive   to take something that is given or sent to you

recent   happening a short time ago

recess   a place set back in a wall. The same word also means a short rest from work or lessons.

recipe (*say ressipee*)   information that tells you how to cook something and what to put in it

recite   to say something aloud that you have learned by heart, like reciting a poem

reckless   careless; not thinking or caring about what could happen

reckon   to count or add up. The same word sometimes means to suppose or consider.

recognize   to know something because you have seen it before

record a disc played on a record-player. The same word means a written account of something that has happened and also the best someone has ever done, like the fastest time for a race.

recorder an instrument you blow into to make musical sounds

record-player an instrument for playing phonograph records

recover to find or get something back, which you have lost. The same word also means to get better after being ill.

recreation something people like to do in their spare time, such as sport or gardening

rectangle a shape with four sides and four right angles

recur to happen again

red a bright color. Fire engines are usually red.

reduce to make something smaller or less in quantity

reed a tall stiff grass that grows in or near water. Reeds are usually hollow.

reef a line of rocks lying just under the water, so that the waves break over it

reek to smell very strongly and usually unpleasantly

reel a lively dance. The same word also means a circular piece of wood or metal on which wire, thread or string is wound.

refer   to mention or speak of: to look up information in a book

referee   someone who has to see that rules are obeyed in games and sports

reflect   to throw back light or heat from a shiny surface

refreshment   a light snack or a drink that makes you feel better when you are tired

refrigerator   a cold box or room where food is stored to keep it fresh

refuge   a shelter

refuse   to say you will not do something you are asked to do

regard   to look at. The same word also means to think well or affectionately of someone.

register   a written list of names or things kept for a special purpose

regret   to feel sorry about something

regular   usual; always happening at the same time

rehearse   to practice for a performance

reign   the period of time that a king or queen rules

reindeer   a kind of large deer that lives in very cold places

reins   leather straps used to guide a horse

rejoice   to feel full of joy; very happy

relation   someone who is connected with your family, like a cousin or an aunt

relative   another word for relation

relax   to rest and take it easy

release   to let go; to set free

relent   to become less angry with someone; to forgive

reliable   able to be trusted

relieve   to give help; to reduce a pain or worry. The same word also means to take over work or duty from someone else.

religion   a belief in God or gods

religious   believing in and worshipping God or gods

rely   to trust or depend on

remain   to stay behind or to be left

remainder   the part left over; the rest of

remark   something someone says

remember   to keep something in your mind always or bring something back into your mind; the opposite of forget

remind   to make someone remember something

remove   to take away or take off

rent   the money you pay for the use of something you do not own, such as a house or machine

repair   to mend; to make right

repeat   to say or do over again

repent   to be sorry for something you have said or done; to regret

replace   to put back

reply   to answer

report   to write or tell about something that has happened. The same word also means the noise when a gun is fired.

represent   to speak or act for someone or something else

reproach   to scold or blame someone for what he has done

reptile   a crawling or creeping cold-blooded scaly animal, such as a snake or a crocodile

request   to ask someone to do something; to ask for something

require   to need

rescue   to save, to take someone away from danger

resemble   to look like someone or something else

reservoir   a man-made lake for storing water

resist   to struggle or fight against someone who is trying to make you do something you don't want to do

resolve   to make up your mind; to decide to do something

respect   to admire or have a very good opinion of someone

responsible   looking after the safe keeping of someone or something

rest   to stop working or playing and be quiet

restaurant   a place where you can buy and eat food

result   whatever happens at the end of some action. For example, if you go out without your coat you may catch cold as a result.

retreat   to go back or run away from danger

return   to come back again or give something back

reveal   to show something that is hidden or secret

revenge   to get your own back on someone who has hurt or injured you

reverse   the opposite; the other way

revolution   the overthrowing of a government by rebels who want another kind of government

revolt   to rebel against authority

revolve   to turn around in a circle

revolver   a kind of pistol

reward   something you get in return for something you have done, such as a prize for winning a race

rhinoceros   a large wild animal with a very thick skin and one or two horns on its snout

rhododendron   an evergreen shrub with large leaves and large, beautifully colored flowers

rhubarb   a plant with thick red stalks that taste good when they are cooked with sugar

rhyme (*say rime*)   words that have the same sound at the end, like *blue*, *zoo* and *shoe*

rhythm (*say rithm*)   a regular pattern or beat of music that you can keep time to

rib   one of the rounded bones between your shoulders and your waist

ribbon   a narrow piece of silky or velvety cloth used to make your hair or your clothes look pretty

rice   the seeds of a food plant that grows in hot countries. Rice grains are hard, but become soft when they are cooked.

rich   having lots of money

rick   a stack or pile of hay

rid   to remove entirely

riddle   a special kind of question. You have to be clever and try to guess the answer.

ride   to be carried on a vehicle or an animal

rider   someone who rides

ridge   a long narrow top of a hill between valleys; a narrow raised strip of something

ridicule   to make fun of or laugh at someone

ridiculous   silly; foolish; laughable

rifle   a long gun

right   the opposite of left and the opposite of wrong. The same word also means the correct and proper thing to say or do.

right angle   an angle of 90 degrees. The corners of a square are all right angles.

rim   the outside edge of something round, like the rim of a wheel

ring   a circle. Some rings are made of gold or silver and pretty stones, to be worn on your fingers. The same word also means the sound of a bell.

ring-master   a man who announces the acts in a circus

rink   a large circle or square of ice that you can skate on

rinse   to take soap away by washing in clear water

riot   a noisy disturbance by a lot of people, often dangerous and violent

rip   to tear something

ripe   ready to eat

ripple   a small wave or movement on the surface of water

rise   to move upwards; to go higher

risk   a chance that you may lose something or be harmed in some way

river   a large amount of water that flows across the land into a lake or sea

road   a hard level surface with no trees or buildings in the way, so that vehicles can get from one place to another

roam to wander about

roar a loud deep noise made by big animals like lions and tigers when they are angry

roast to cook meat in an oven

rob to take something that is not yours; to steal by force

robber someone who steals by force

robe a long garment that covers you down to your ankles

robin a kind of thrush with a reddish breast, sometimes called robin redbreast

rock a large piece of stone. The same word also means to move back and forth or from side to side.

rocket a machine that is shot up into space, sometimes carrying astronauts

rod a long thin stick or bar, usually of wood or metal

rogue a person who is dishonest; a cheat

roll to move along by turning over and over. The same word also means a kind of bread.

roller a machine which rolls to move along, or to make things flat and smooth. The same word also means a hair curler.

roller-skates skates with wheels

rolling-pin a tube-shaped piece of wood or metal used to flatten dough or pastry before it is cooked

roof the covering on top of a building or car

rook a black bird like a crow. It has a hoarse loud cry.

room a part of the inside of a house such as a bedroom or kitchen

rooster an adult male chicken; a cock

root the part of a plant or tree that grows underground

rope very thick string. It is used to tie heavy things together.

rose a beautiful sweet-smelling flower with a prickly stem

rosy pinky-red color

rot to go bad or decay

rotten bad, spoiled. Apples go rotten if they are kept too long.

rough not smooth; bumpy

round curved like a circle

roundabout another word for merry-go-round. The same word also means not direct, not following the straightest way.

rouse to awaken or to stir up somebody's feelings

route (*say root*)   the exact way you go to get from one place to another

rove   to roam or wander about

rover   someone who doesn't stay in one home for very long, but wanders from place to place

row (*rhymes with no*)   a line of things or people. The same word also means to move a boat through water, using oars.

row (*rhymes with now*)   a noisy quarrel or fight

royal   to do with a king or queen

rub   to move something against something else, such as rubbing polish on furniture with a cloth

rubber   a material that stretches or bounces. The same word also means something that takes away pencil marks.

rubbish   something worn out or of no value that you throw away. The same word also means nonsense.

ruby   a jewel, deep red in color

rudder   a piece of wood or metal at the back of a boat or airplane, used for steering

rude   the opposite of polite; bad-mannered. The same word sometimes means rough.

rug   a small floor mat or carpet. The same word also means a kind of blanket used when traveling.

rugged   rough and strong

ruin   to spoil or destroy; to make something useless. The same word also means an old building that is falling down.

rule   what you must or must not do. You must
obey the rules at school. The same word also
means a ruler for measuring.

ruler   a straight piece of wood used for measuring
things. The same word also means a man or
woman who is the head of a country.

rum   a strong drink made from sugar cane

rumble   a low-pitched, deep rolling sound, like
far-away thunder

rumor   something said about a person or events
that may or may not be true

rumpus   a disturbance

run   to move quickly on your feet

rung   a piece of metal or wood used as a step
in a ladder

rural   to do with the country; the opposite of
urban

rush   to hurry; to move quickly to get somewhere
on time. The same word also means a tall
kind of grass growing near water.

rust   a reddish-brown coating that appears on
things made of iron or steel after they
have been in water or out in damp air for
some time

rustle   a soft whispering sound, such as is made by
dry leaves rubbing together

rut   a deep track made by a wheel in soft ground

rye   a kind of grain

sack   a large bag made of cloth, paper or plastic

sacred   holy

sad   not happy; feeling sorry

saddle   a leather seat for a rider, which is fastened
on to a horse's back or a bicycle

safari   an expedition in Africa in search of wild
animals

safe   not able to hurt you; out of danger. The same
word also means a very strong metal box used
to lock money and valuable things away safely.

safety   freedom from harm or danger

sag   to sink down or bend in the middle; to hang
limply or droop

saga   a long story about people and legends of olden
days; a long story about a family and their
family before them

sail   a piece of canvas fastened to a ship's mast.
Sails catch the wind so that the ship is moved
along.

sailor   a man who works on a ship

saint   a very good and holy person

salad   a mixture of cold vegetables, such as lettuce,
tomatoes and beets. Often cold meat, fish
or eggs are added to salads, and some
salads have fruit in them.

salary   money paid regularly, usually every week or
month, for work done

sale the exchange of something for money. The same word also means a period when shops sell some of their goods more cheaply.

saliva the liquid that keeps the inside of your mouth moist

salmon a large fish with silvery scales and pink flesh

salt a white powder we get from the earth and from sea water. It is used in cooking or at meals to make food taste better.

salute to greet someone, usually by raising your right hand to your forehead

same not different; like something else

sample one of, or a small part of something that shows what the rest of it is like

sand small grains of rock which we find in large quantities at the seaside or in the desert

sandal a light shoe, held on the foot by straps

sandwich two pieces of bread with meat or some other food between them

sap the juice in plants and trees

sardine a small fish, usually sold in tins

sari a long piece of cloth wrapped around the body and hanging loose over the shoulder, worn by girls and women in India

sash a strip of ribbon or cloth worn round the waist or over the shoulder. The same word also means the frame of a window that slides up and down.

satchel a bag, used for carrying school books

satellite a planet that revolves around another larger planet, as the moon revolves around the earth

satin a soft shiny material

satisfactory good enough; pleasing

satisfy to do all you can to please someone, or to fill a need

sauce liquid poured over food to give it more flavor. Mint sauce is used with roast lamb.

saucepan a cooking pot with a lid and a handle

saucer a small curved plate put under a cup

saucy a bit impudent

sausage a meat mixture chopped up very small and put into a thin bag made of animal skin

savage fierce and cruel; wild

save to keep something to use later on. The same word also means to help someone who is in danger.

saw a metal tool with pointed teeth on one edge, used for cutting wood

sawdust powder from wood that has been sawn

say to speak; to tell something

saying a thing that is often said, like *A stitch in time saves nine*

scab the dry crust on a sore place or wound when it begins to heal

scabbard a case or holder for a sword; a sheath

scald to burn yourself with a very hot liquid or steam

scale one of the small horny flakes that cover the skin of snakes and fishes. The same word also means a set of notes in music.

scales a weighing machine

scar the mark left on your skin after a sore or wound has healed

scarce not enough; difficult to find

scarcely hardly; not quite

scarcity a very small supply of something, so that there is not enough to go round

scarecrow something, usually like the dummy figure of a man, which is put in a field to frighten the birds away from the crops

scared afraid

scarf a long thick piece of material you wear to keep your neck warm

scarlet bright red

scatter to throw things around in all directions, like scattering bread crumbs on the ground for birds to eat

scene a view: the place where something happens: part of a play

scenery what you see when you look around you, such as hills and fields and trees in the country. The same word also means the painted curtains and other things used on a stage to make it look like a real place.

scent a smell. The same word also means a liquid with a sweet pleasant smell; a perfume.

scholar   a person who studies; a pupil or student

scholarship   knowledge or learning. The same word also means a sum of money given to a student each year because of his good work, so that he can afford to go on studying.

school   a place where people go to learn

schooner   a large sailing ship

science   knowledge got by careful study and testing of things, often to do with nature. Chemistry is a natural science.

scientific   to do with science. When you study chemistry you do scientific experiments.

scientist   someone who finds out why things happen on earth and in space

scissors   a cutting tool like two knives fastened together in the middle

scold   to speak crossly to someone about something he has done

scoop   a tool shaped like a deep shovel, that is used to dig up earth or sand. Small scoops are used to measure out dry foods, such as sugar, shelled nuts and flour.

scoot   to move away quickly

scooter   a small two-wheeled vehicle, moved by pushing with one foot or by an engine

scorch to burn slightly; to dry up with heat. Anything that has been scorched turns a yellow-brown color

score the number of points, goals or marks you get in a game or in an examination

scorn to think that something or someone is not worth bothering about, or no good

scout someone sent to spy on the enemy: a member of the Boy Scouts

scowl to frown

scramble to climb up on rough ground, usually using your hands and feet

scrap a small piece of something. The same word also means to quarrel or fight.

scrape to rub against something with a rough or sharp edge

scratch a mark made with something sharp. The same word also means to scrape with fingernails or claws.

scrawl to write in an untidy way that is not easy to read

scream a very loud high-pitched cry of surprise, pain or fear

screech a piercing scream

screen a light-weight wall that you can move around. The same word also means what a television or moving picture is shown on. The word also means a window covering used to keep insects out.

screw a special kind of thick nail with grooves. You turn it round and round with a tool called a screwdriver to make it go into wood.

scribble to write in a careless and untidy way

script handwriting, or printing that looks like handwriting

scrub to rub something, usually with a brush, to get it clean

sculpture the art of carving stone and wood, or modeling clay or metal into statues and beautiful designs

scurry to hurry along in a bustling way

sea the salty water that covers parts of the earth where there is no land

seagull a sea bird, usually colored gray and white. It makes a loud screeching sound.

seahorse a pretty little sea animal with no legs. Its body ends in a curly tail to help it swim along in an upright position.

seal a fish-eating animal that can also live on land. The same word also means to close or fasten something, so that it cannot be opened without breaking the fastening.

sea lion a large kind of seal. The male makes a roaring noise, like a lion.

seam a line where two pieces of material are joined together by sewing

seaplane   an airplane that can take off from or land on the sea

search   to look everywhere for something

searchlight   a very powerful beam of light that shows things clearly in the dark

seashell   the hard covering on some kinds of fish and sea animals

seaside   a place by the sea, where you can go for your holidays

season   spring, summer, autumn and winter are the four seasons of the year. The same word also means to add things like salt and pepper to food to improve the flavor.

seat   a piece of furniture for sitting on

seaweed   plants that grow in the sea

second   next after first. The same word also means a measurement of time. There are 60 seconds in a minute.

secondary   next after primary; second in importance

secret   something known only to you or to a very few other people

secretary   someone who writes or types business letters in an office

section   a part or a piece of something

secure   safe; fastened tightly

see   to use your eyes to look at something

seed   the part of the plant from which new plants grow

seek   to look for

see-saw   a strong board fastened in the middle to a heavy piece of wood or metal. Two people can sit on it, one on each end, and go up and down in turn.

seize   to grasp and hold on to

seldom   not often

select   to choose

self   your own person

selfish   thinking only of yourself, and not caring much about other people's wishes

sell   to give something in exchange for money

semi-circle   a half circle

semolina   small hard particles of wheat, usually cooked in a pudding

send   to make a person or thing go somewhere

senior   someone who is older or more important than others

sensation   a feeling

sense   good or right knowledge. The same word also means being able to tell what things are like by tasting, smelling, touching, seeing or hearing.

senseless   foolish; without good sense. The same word also means not to be conscious of what is going on around you.

sensible   wise; having good sense

sentence   a number of words that make a complete thought when put together. The same word also means a punishment for breaking the law.

sentry   a soldier who keeps guard

separate   not joined together; divided

sequin   a small round shiny ornament sewn on clothing to make it sparkle

sergeant   an officer in the army or police

serial   a story or film that appears in parts and not all at one time

series   a number of things or events following one another in regular order

serious   not foolish or making fun; deeply thoughtful. The same word also means causing worry, as when someone has a serious illness.

serpent   another word for snake

servant   someone who is paid to work in someone else's house

serve   to work for someone; to hand out food at meals; to sell things over the counter in a shop

settee   a long seat with a back and arms, with room for several people to sit

settle   to agree upon something, such as settling on a day to go out with someone

several   more than two of something; a few

severe   very serious: not merciful

sew   to join cloth together with a needle and thread

sex   either of the two groups, male and female, that animals and humans are divided into

shabby   nearly worn out; almost ragged. The same word also means not fair or kind, as when someone plays a shabby trick on you.

shade   to keep the light away from something

shadow   a dark shape that appears on the ground when an object gets in the way of light

shaggy   covered with rough long hair or fur, usually untidy

shake   to move something quickly up and down or from side to side

shallow   the opposite of deep; not very far to the bottom

shame   a feeling of unhappiness because you have hurt someone or done something you know is wrong

shameful   wrong; mean

shampoo   to wash your hair

shamrock   a kind of clover plant with tiny leaves divided into three sections

shape   what something is like if you draw a line around the outside of it. A ball is shaped like a circle.

share   to give part of something to someone else

shark   a large dangerous sea fish, which has very sharp teeth

sharp   having an edge that can cut or a point that can make holes

shatter   to break something into many pieces

shave   to cut off hair with a razor

shawl   a square piece of cloth folded and worn around the head and shoulders by girls and women

sheaf   a bundle (of wheat) or a bunch (of papers)

shears   large scissors, used for cutting things like hedges or sheep's wool

sheath   a scabbard; a cover for the blade of a sword or knife

shed   a hut made of wood or metal, often used to keep tools in

sheep   an animal covered with thick wool

sheet   a large piece of cloth used on a bed. The same word also means a single piece of paper, glass or metal.

shelf   a board fastened to a wall. You can keep books and other things on it.

shell   the hard covering on a nut or egg. Some fish, animals and insects also have shells.

shelter   a place where you are safe from danger or from bad weather

shepherd   a man who looks after sheep

sheriff   the chief government officer in a county or district

shield   something you hide behind or hold up to protect yourself from attack

shift to move something, usually something heavy. The same word also means a group of people working together for a number of hours, such as a night shift.

shimmer to shine with a soft and trembling light

shine to give out bright light. Silver and gold are shiny; a torch shines in the dark.

shingle one of the flat pieces of wood used like slates to cover a roof

ship a very large boat that goes across the ocean

shipwreck a ship that has been sunk or destroyed, usually by a storm at sea

shirt a piece of clothing worn on the upper part of the body by men and boys

shiver to shake because you are cold or because you are afraid

shock a nasty surprise

shoe a covering for your foot

shoot to send a bullet from a gun, or an arrow from a bow

shop a place where you can buy things

shore land at the edge of a lake or the sea

short not very long; not very tall

shorthand a quick way of writing down what is said

shot small bullets for a shotgun

shoulder   the joint between your arm and body

shout   to speak or call out very loudly

shove   to push roughly

shovel   a tool like a spade, but wider

show   to point out; to guide. The same word also means a spectacle.

shower   a sudden brief fall of rain, sleet or snow. The same word also means a bath in which you stand up and water sprays all over you.

shred   a scrap or strip torn off something

shriek   a high-pitched scream; a shrill laugh

shrill   high-pitched and piercing to the ears

shrimp   a small gray shellfish that turns pink when cooked

shrink   to become less or smaller. Some kinds of cloth shrink when they have been washed.

shrivel   to dry up and become smaller. A raisin is a shriveled grape.

shrub   a small woody plant that doesn't grow very tall; a bush

shudder   to shiver or tremble with fear or disgust

shuffle   to move your feet along without lifting them. The same word also means to mix a pack of cards before playing a game.

shut   closed, not open

shutter   a wooden cover for a window, used to keep heat and light out in daytime, and to keep burglars out at night

shuttlecock   a toy made of feathers stuck in a cork, used in the game of badminton

shy   not wanting to be with lots of other people

sick   ill, not well

sideboard   a large, heavy piece of furniture like a cupboard, where dishes, table linen and cutlery are kept

siege   an attempt to capture a town or fort by surrounding it, so that help cannot reach it

sieve   a container with many small holes, used to separate large and small lumps of soil, grain or food

sift   to separate grains or powder from larger lumps by means of a sieve

sigh   to breathe out heavily when you are tired or sad

sight   the ability to see

sign   a movement to show what you mean, like nodding your head to mean *yes*. The same word also means a mark or notice that tells you something, like a traffic sign.

signal   a message sent by signs

silent   not making a sound

silk   very fine smooth cloth made from threads that silkworms spin

silkworm a caterpillar that spins silk threads

sill the wooden or stone ledge at the bottom of a door or window

silly not clever; not thinking carefully

silver a shiny grayish-white metal. Money, knives, forks and spoons are sometimes made of silver. The same word also means the color of the metal.

similar like, or almost like something else

simple easy, not difficult. The same word also means foolish, not very clever.

since from a certain time until now, as when you say you have had nothing to eat since breakfast

sincere honest; meaning what you say

sing to make music with your voice

singe (*say sinj*) to burn slightly, to scorch

single only one. The same word also means not married.

singular one only, not plural. The same word also means unusual, extraordinary.

sink a place in the kitchen where there is running water for washing dishes and preparing vegetables. The same word also means to go under the water.

sip to drink something a little bit at a time

siren an instrument or whistle that makes a loud, wailing noise

sister a daughter of the same parents

sit to be on a chair or seat

site an area of ground where a building is, or will be built

situation the place or position of something. The same word also means a job.

size the amount of space something takes up

skate a metal blade or wheels fastened on a shoe, so that you can move quickly and smoothly on ice or a flat surface. The same word also means a large flat fish with very wide fins.

skeleton all the bones inside your body

sketch a rough quick drawing

ski (*say skee*) to move quickly over hard snow on two long pieces of wood called skis, which are fastened to your boots

skid to slide sideways, as a car sometimes does on wet or icy roads

skill cleverness; the ability to do something well

skillful clever: able to do something well

skim to glide quickly over the surface of something. The same word also means to take the cream off the top of the milk.

skin the outside covering of your body

skip   to jump up and down on one leg at a time, often over a rope. The same word also means to leave out something, like skipping dull parts of a book.

skipper   the captain of a ship

skirt   a garment that hangs down from the waist; the part of a dress that hangs down from the waist

skull   the bony part of your head

skunk   a small black animal with white stripes and a bushy tail. It gives out a very bad-smelling liquid when it is in danger.

sky   the air above you that you see when you look up out of doors

skylark   a lark, a small bird which sings when it is flying very high up in the air

skyscraper   a very tall building

slab   a thick slice

slack   loose; not tightly stretched. The same word also means careless or neglectful.

slam   to shut or bang something with a loud noise

slanting   not straight up and down; sloping, like this line /

slap   to hit with the palm of the hand

slash   to make long cuts in something, sometimes violently

slate   a kind of stone used for roofs

slaughter   killing of animals, usually for food: a terrible killing of one person or great numbers of people

slave   someone who is not free because he is owned by another person and has to work for him

slay   to kill

sled   a vehicle with metal or wooden runners, that moves easily over snow-covered ground

sledge   a sled

sleek   smooth and shiny, like the coat of a horse which has been well fed and cared for

sleep   You sleep when you are not awake.

sleet   rain mixed with snow or hail

sleeve   the part of your clothes that covers your arm

sleeveless   without sleeves

sleigh   a large sled, usually pulled by horses

slender   slim; narrow; not looking strong or heavy

slice   a flat piece cut from something, like a slice of bread or cake

slide   to move smoothly down or along on something

slight   small in quantity or importance; slim or slender

slightly   by a small amount

slim   thin; narrow; not fat

slime   thin slippery mud or dirt

sling   a piece of cloth tied around your neck and shoulder to hold up a broken or injured arm

slingshot   a Y-shaped stick with elastic attached, used for shooting stones

slip   to slide when you don't mean to

slipper   a soft shoe you wear indoors

slippery   smooth on the surface so that you slip in walking, as on ice or thin mud

slit   a long thin cut

slop   to spill

slope   ground that goes upwards or downwards; slanting; not straight

slot   a narrow opening in a machine for a coin

slouch   to walk or move in a lazy droopy way, not holding yourself up straight

slow   the opposite of fast. To be slow is to take a long time to do something.

sludge   nasty soft mud

slug   a large kind of snail without a shell

slush   melting snow; soft mud

sly   cunning; artful

smack   to hit with the open hand; to slap

small   another word for little; the opposite of large

smart   clever; quick to learn: well dressed, stylish

smash   to break something into pieces, usually with a crashing noise

smear   to spread or rub something greasy or sticky so as to leave a dirty mark

smell   what your nose tells you about something

smile   to look happy

smith   a man who makes things out of metal, like a silversmith or blacksmith

smock   a loose garment, usually worn over other clothes to keep them clean

smoke   the cloud of tiny particles that comes from something burning

smolder   to burn slowly without much flame

smooth   without any bumps; the opposite of rough

smother   to cover completely: to stop someone breathing by covering his mouth and nose

smudge   a stain, a smear of dirt

smuggle   to bring something secretly into one country from another without paying tax

snack   a small quick meal, like a sandwich or biscuits and cheese

snail   a small animal that moves very slowly. It has a shell on its back.

snake a crawling animal with a long body and no legs. Some snakes are dangerous because they have a poisonous bite.

snap to break with a sudden sharp noise

snarl to make a growling noise, with the teeth showing. The same word also means a knot or tangle.

snatch to grab something quickly

sneak to tell tales about someone behind his back: to creep along quietly

sneer to smile in a scornful or mocking way

sneeze to make a sudden blowing noise through your nose because it tickles

sniff to take in a noisy breath through your nose

snip to cut a little piece off something, usually with scissors

snore to make a loud breathing noise through your mouth when you are asleep

snorkel a tube with one end sticking out of the water so that swimmers can stay under and still keep breathing air

snout the sticking-out nose and mouth of some animals such as pigs and porpoises

snow drops of water that become frozen in the air in winter. The pieces that float down through the air are called snowflakes.

snowball   a ball of snow pressed together

snowman   a man made out of snow

snowshoe   one of a pair of frames strung with thin strips of leather. People wear snowshoes to keep their feet from sinking into deep soft snow.

snug   cosy and warm

soak   to make something or someone very wet

soap   something you use with water to make things clean

soar   to fly high into the air

sob   to weep noisily

sock   a short stocking you put on to cover your feet and ankles before you put on your shoes

socket   a hollow place that you fit something into, like a socket for an electric bulb

sofa   another word for couch

soft   not hard, rough or loud

soggy   damp and heavy; very wet

soil   loose earth. The same word also means to make something dirty.

solar   having to do with the sun

soldier   a man in the army

sole   the bottom of your foot or your shoe. The same word also means a kind of flat fish.

solemn   serious; very earnest

solid   hard and firm all through, not hollow or liquid

solitary   alone; by yourself

solve   to find the answer to something puzzling or difficult

some   a few; not all

somebody   a person who is not named

someone   another word for somebody

somersault   to go head over heels

sometime   at a time not known

sometimes   not all the time; now and then

something   a thing not named

somewhat   rather; a little

somewhere   at an unknown place

son   a male child of a father or mother

song   words and music together, which you sing. The same word also means the musical notes sung by birds.

sonic   having to do with sound waves, as in sonic boom

soon   in a short time

soot   a soft black powdery stuff which comes from burning wood or coal. It sticks to the inside of the chimney.

soothe   to calm someone down; to comfort

sore painful when touched

sorrow unhappiness; sadness

sorry feeling unhappy about something you have
 done, or something that has happened

sort to put together things that belong
 together

soul the invisible part of a person which is
 believed to live on after death

sound anything that can be heard

soup a liquid food made by boiling meat,
 vegetables or other foods together in water

sour not sweet tasting. Lemons taste sour.

source the beginning or starting place of something,
 like a stream or river

south the direction opposite to north, on your
 right as you face the rising sun

sow (*rhymes with no*) to scatter seed over the
 ground or plant it in the ground

sow (*rhymes with now*) a female pig

space a place with nothing in it. The same word is
 often used to mean the sky higher than
 airplanes can fly, where there is not even any
 air.

spaceship a special machine moved by rocket
 motors that can go far
 up into space to
 the moon and beyond

spade　a tool used for digging in the ground

spaghetti　long tubes of dried wheat paste, like macaroni only much longer and thinner

span　the distance between the tip of your thumb and little finger when your hand is stretched out. The same word also means the length of anything from end to end.

spangle　a thin piece of shiny metal sewn on to a garment. Lots of spangles sewn on to a dress make it glitter and sparkle.

spaniel　a kind of dog with a silky coat and long floppy ears

spank　to smack with your open hand

spare　to let something go. The same word also means extra. If you have two copies of the same book, one of them is a spare copy.

spark　a tiny bit of something burning, that flies out of the fire

sparkle　to give off bright flashes of light; to glitter. Snow sparkles in the sunlight.

sparkler　a firework which gives off silver or colored sparks when you light it

sparrow　a small brown and gray bird

speak　to say something

spear　a pole with a metal point on the end. It is used as a weapon.

special　not like anything else; made for one use only

specimen　one of something; a sample

speck   a small spot or dirty mark; a tiny piece

speckled   marked with lots of small spots

spectacle   something interesting which makes people want to look at it

spectacles   another word for the glasses people wear to help them to see better

spectator   someone who looks on or watches others doing something

speech   the act of speaking. The same word also means a talk or lecture.

speed   quickness, swiftness

spell   to put letters together in the right order to make up a certain word. The same word also means magic words which are supposed to make something happen.

spend   to pay out money

spice   dried or powdered flavorings for food, usually tasting and smelling strongly

spider   a small animal with eight legs. It spins a web to catch insects.

spike   a long sharp point. The same word also means an ear of grain or a tall cluster of flowers on a stem.

spill   to let something, such as powder or liquid accidentally run out from a container

spin   to go round and round. The same word also means to make thread out of raw wool, cotton or flax.

spinach a dark green leafy vegetable

spindle a thin rod on which thread is twisted in spinning

spine the backbone of a person or animal. The same word also means a thorn, or one of the thin, stiff prickles growing on some animals, such as hedgehogs.

spinster an unmarried woman

spiral something that winds upwards, going round and round in continuous curves

spire the long pointed top of a church steeple

spirit another word for soul; a ghost

spit to throw out something from your mouth

spite a wish to be cruel to someone or to hurt his feelings

spiteful saying and doing cruel things to someone you don't like

splash the noise of something heavy falling into liquid. The same word also means to throw liquid about.

splashdown the landing of a space capsule in the ocean

splendid wonderful; very rich and grand; very good

splinter a tiny thin piece of wood, glass or metal, which has broken off from a larger piece

split to break or cut something from end to end

spoil to damage something or make it of no use. The same word also means to give a child his own way too much.

sponge   the soft, yellowish skeleton of a sea animal, which becomes much softer when it soaks up water. It is used for washing yourself. The same word also means a kind of soft cake.

spool   a reel on which you wind things like thread, ribbon, or film

spoon   a tool used in cooking and eating food

sport   a game, usually played outdoors. Football and baseball are sports.

spot   a small mark

spout   a small tube or pipe through which liquid is poured, like the spout of a teapot

sprain   to twist a joint or muscle so badly that it swells

sprawl   to sit or lie in a relaxed position, with your arms and legs spread out

spray   to send out fine drops of liquid

spread   to cover a surface, like spreading butter on bread

spring   to move quickly and suddenly. The same word also means a piece of metal which can be pressed down but jumps back into position when you let it go. The word also means the season after winter, when plants begin to grow.

sprinkle   to scatter small drops of water or bits of something, like sugar or sawdust

sprout   to begin to grow. The same word also means a green vegetable like a tiny cabbage. Its full name is a brussels sprout.

spurt   to squirt out suddenly; a rush of liquid

spy   someone who secretly watches what other people are doing, especially during a war when he is paid to get information about the enemy

square   a rectangle whose four sides are equal in length

squash   to crush or squeeze something out of shape. The same word also means a large green or yellow fruit that grows on a vine.

squaw   an American Indian woman

squeak   a small high sound. A mouse squeaks and so does a rusty door hinge.

squeal   a long high piercing sound made by some animals

squeeze   to press hard; to crush; to hug

squirrel   a small red or gray animal with a long bushy tail

squirt   to force liquid out of an opening in a sudden stream; to spurt

stab   to pierce or cut with a pointed weapon

stable   a building where horses are kept

stack   a large heap

stadium   an open-air sports field with rows of seats all round

staff   a group of people working together, like people in an office, or teachers in a school. The same word also means a pole or stick carried in the hand.

stag   a male deer

stage   the platform in a theatre or hall where people act, sing, or speak

stage coach   a horse-drawn coach which traveled across the country in olden days, stopping at certain places to let people off or on

stagger   to walk unsteadily, lurching and stumbling

stain   a dirty mark

staircase   a number of stairs, usually with a side-rail to keep you from falling

stairs   a set of steps in a building for walking up or down

stake   a strong pointed stick or post

stale   not fresh; dry and without much taste because of being kept too long

stalk   another word for stem. The same word also means to creep quietly after an animal that you are hunting.

stall   a kind of table on which things for sale are shown at a market. The same word also means a place for one animal in a cattle shed or stable.

stallion   a male horse

stammer   to repeat the beginning of a word several times before going on to say the whole word; to speak in jerks and pauses

stamp   a little piece of colored paper you stick on a letter or parcel, which pays for sending it by mail. The same word also means to hit the floor hard with the sole of your foot.

stand   to be on your feet; not sitting. The same word also means rows of raised seats for people watching an outdoor game.

standard   a flag or banner

star   a tiny light which shines in the night sky. The same word also means someone who is famous and popular, like a film star.

stare   to look at something or someone for a long time without looking away

starfish   a flat sea animal with five arms like the points of a star

starling   a wild bird with glossy, dark greenish-purple feathers, speckled with white

start   to begin; to move suddenly

startle   to make a person or animal start with sudden fear or surprise

starvation   suffering or death caused by lack of food

starve   to be in great need of food; to die of hunger

statement   something said or told

station   the place where a train stops to let people on or off. The same word also means a building for policemen or firemen.

stationary   not moving; standing still

stationery   writing paper and envelopes

statue   the figure of a person or animal which is carved from stone or wood. Sometimes statues are made of metal or some other material.

stay   to be in one place and not leave

steadily   in a steady, firm way

steady   standing firm; moving without jerking or shaking. The same word also means loyal and faithful.

steak   a thick slice of meat or fish

steal   to take something which belongs to someone else

steam   the cloud-like gas that water turns into when it boils

steel   a very strong metal made from iron

steep   rising nearly straight up from the ground, like a steep hill

steeple   a high pointed tower on a church

steer   to guide a vehicle or ship to the right or left. The same word also means a young bull.

stellar   having to do with the stars

stem   the thin part of a plant that holds up the flowers or leaves

step   to put one foot in front of the other when walking. The same word also means one stair in a staircase.

stern severe; strict; grim. The same word also means the back part of a ship or boat.

stew to cook food, especially meat with vegetables, by boiling it slowly

stick a long thin piece of wood: anything shaped like a stick, such as a stick of wax or gum

sticky clinging or holding on, as when something like glue or honey sticks to your fingers

stiff firm; hard; not easily bent or moved

stile a little set of steps fixed to a fence or a wall to help you climb over

still not moving; calm

stilt one of a pair of tall poles with foot rests

sting the sharp part of an insect, like a pin, which can hurt you

stir to move; to shake up or mix

stirrup a metal ring hanging down each side of a saddle. It is flat at the bottom so that you can put your foot in it when you ride a horse.

stitch a loop of thread that has been sewn. The same word also means a sudden sharp pain in your side, usually caused by running.

stock supplies of food and other goods stored by shop-keepers

stocking a kind of sock that covers the whole of your leg. Stockings are usually made of nylon, wool or silk.

stoke to put fuel on the fire to make it hotter

stole a long, narrow piece of material, often made of fur or silk, worn over the shoulders and hanging down

stomach a kind of pocket in the middle of your body, which holds food after it has been swallowed

stone a small piece of rock. The same word also means the hard seed inside some fruit like plums and cherries.

stool a little seat with no back or arms

stoop to bend the upper part of your body downwards

stop to end or leave off what you are doing

stopper something you put in the neck of a bottle to close the opening

store to keep something until it is needed. The same word also means a shop.

stork a large bird with very long legs and a long beak

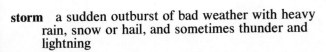

storm a sudden outburst of bad weather with heavy rain, snow or hail, and sometimes thunder and lightning

story an adventure told or written. It can be a true story, or made up like a fairy tale.

stove something which makes heat for us to cook food or warm the room

straight not crooked or curved. This is a straight line _____

straighten to make straight; to put things neat and tidy

strain to make every effort; to put all your strength into doing something

strainer a kind of bowl with holes in it, usually made of metal or plastic. You put vegetables or other food in it to let the water out.

strange unusual; out of place

stranger someone you do not know

strangle to kill a person or animal by squeezing its throat; to choke

strap a long thin piece of leather, usually with a buckle, to fasten something

straw dry stiff yellow stalks that farm animals like to sleep on

strawberry a small soft red fruit with a lot of seeds

stray to wander away or go in the wrong direction by mistake

streak a stripe or long narrow mark

stream a small river

streamer a long thin flag, or a paper decoration for parties

street a road with houses or other buildings on both sides of it

strength how strong or powerful something is

stretch to make longer or wider by pulling

strict insisting on complete obedience without exception; severe; stern

stride   to walk with long steps

strike   to hit someone or something as hard as you can. The same word also means to stop work because the workers want more money or because they think some things at work could be much better.

string   a long piece of thick thread for tying up things: one of the parts of a musical instrument, such as a violin or guitar

strip   a long narrow piece of something. The same word also means to take off all your clothes.

stripe   a long narrow line or mark of color, usually in material. Flags often have different colored stripes on them.

stroke   to rub gently, as you would stroke a cat. The same word also means a blow, or the sound of a clock striking.

stroll   to walk slowly, in no hurry to get anywhere

strong   not weak or easily broken: able to lift heavy things

structure   something constructed, like a dam or a building: the way things are built up or arranged

struggle   to make a great effort; to fight to get free

stubborn   not willing to give way to others; obstinate

stud   a kind of fastening for a shirt

student   someone who studies, usually at a college or university

studio   the workshop of an artist: a place where films are made: a room from which radio or television programs are broadcast

study   to learn; to examine something closely

stuff   the material something is made of. The same word also means to pack tightly.

stuffy   without enough fresh air

stumble   to trip over something or lose your footing

stump   the part of a tree trunk that is left after the tree has been cut down

stun   to knock someone senseless; to amaze or surprise greatly

stupid   foolish; silly; slow to think

sturdy   strong; healthy

stutter   to speak with difficulty because you find it hard to get words out easily; to stammer

sty   a place where pigs are kept. The same word also means a small swelling on the eyelid.

style   the way something is done, such as old-style dancing, the newest style of clothes, or good style in writing

subject   a person who is ruled by the head of a country. The same word also means what is being talked or written about—for example, *The subject of the talk was sport.*

submarine   a special kind of ship that can go along under water

substance   anything solid that you can handle or feel: the main part of something

subtract to take away a number or a quantity from a larger number or quantity

subway an underground electric train; an underground passage for pedestrians

succeed to do what you set out to do. The same word also means to come after, or to follow in order, as when a prince becomes king by succeeding his father.

success a satisfactory ending to something you set out to do, like success in passing an examination or winning a race

suck to draw liquid into your mouth; to keep something in your mouth without chewing it

sudden happening all at once

suddenly unexpectedly; all at once

suds soapy bubbles

suede a soft leather which doesn't shine

suet a kind of hard fat taken from sheep and cattle and used in cooking

suffer to feel pain; to put up with

sufficient enough

sugar a white substance used in food and drinks to make them taste sweet

sugar cane a plant with sweet-tasting stems from which sugar is made

suggest to tell others about an idea or plan that you think would be good

suit a set of clothes, such as a coat and trousers, which are meant to be worn together

suitable fitting in well; proper; right

suitcase a flat case for carrying clothes when you are going away

suite (*say sweet*) a set of rooms at an hotel or large house. The same word also means a set of furniture for a room.

sulk to show you are angry and bad-tempered by not speaking and not being friendly

sum the total number when two or more things are added together

summarize to go over the main points of what you have been saying or writing

summer the warmest season of the year, between spring and autumn

summit the highest point of something, such as the summit of a mountain

sun the round bright ball seen in the sky during the day. It sends out light and heat.

sunburn burning or reddening of the skin when you have been too long in the hot sun

sundial an instrument that shows the time of day by the position of the sun's shadow on a dial

sunny full of sunshine

sunrise the time when the sun comes up: the actual rising of the sun

sunset the time when the sun goes down: the actual setting of the sun

sunshine the light from the sun

supermarket   a large shop where you can buy all kinds of food and some other things as well. You help yourself and pay when you go out.

supersonic   moving faster than sound travels in air

supper   the last meal before you go to bed

supply   to provide; to give something that is needed

support   to hold something up; to bear the weight of something

suppose   to imagine; to pretend

sure   knowing you are right

surely   without question or doubt

surface   the outside of anything; the top of a lake or the sea or the earth

surgeon   a doctor who cures patients by cutting out or repairing diseased parts of the body

surgery   curing illness by cutting out or repairing the diseased part

surly   bad-tempered; not friendly

surname   your last name; the family name

surprise   something you don't expect

surrender   to give up

surround   to be all around; on all sides of something

survey   to take a careful look over something or some place

suspect   to have a feeling in your mind that something is wrong or that someone is not telling the truth

swallow   to let food or drink go down your throat. The same word also means a pretty dark blue and white bird with a forked tail.

swamp   wet, marshy ground. The same word also means to put too much water in something.

swan   a large water-bird with a very long neck. It is usually white.

swap   to exchange something for something else

swarm   a large number of insects, animals or people moving together

sway   to swing or move from side to side

swear   to make a very solemn promise. The same word also means to use bad language.

sweat   the moisture that comes from your skin when you are hot

sweater   a knitted jersey

sweep   to use a brush or broom to clean the floor

sweet   tasting of sugar; not sour

sweetheart   someone you love and hope to marry

swell   to grow larger or louder

swerve   to turn aside quickly, as when you swerve so as not to bump into something when you are running

swift   fast; quick; rapid. The same word also means a bird with long pointed wings that can fly very fast.

swill   to drink in large amounts. The same word also means pigs' food.

swim   to move along in the water using your arms and legs

swing   a seat hanging from ropes or chains. The same word also means to move in the air, back and forth, or from side to side.

swipe   to hit hard and rather wildly

swirl   to move about quickly with a circling movement, as when dried leaves are blown about by the wind

switch   a little lever which turns on electricity

swollen   made bigger by swelling

sword   a very long knife with a special handle, used for fighting or for carrying in some ceremonies

syllable   a group of sounds that make a word or part of a word. The words *boy* and *girl* each have one syllable, the words *women* and *children* have two syllables.

sympathy   a feeling of kindness and pity towards someone who is sad or ill

syrup   a thick sweet liquid made by boiling sugar with water or fruit juice

system   a group of things working together

tab   a small flap or loop, usually on a piece of clothing

table   a piece of furniture with legs and a flat top. The same word also means a set of facts or figures arranged in columns.

tablecloth   a large piece of material used to cover a table

tablet   a small, flat piece of something, like stone, soap and some kinds of medicine

tack   a short nail with a wide flat head. The same word also means to sew something together with long loose stitches.

tackle   to use all your strength to try to do something. The same word also means the equipment for doing something, such as fishing tackle.

tadpole   a frog when it is very young, before its legs develop

taffeta   a kind of stiff shiny cloth used for making dresses

tag   a label. The same word also means a children's game in which one person chases and tries to touch another.

tail   the part that comes out at the end of anything, like the tail of an animal, a kite or an airplane

tailor   a man who makes clothes, such as suits, overcoats, skirts and trousers

take   to get hold of: to carry away

tale   another word for a story

talk   to speak or say something

talkative   fond of talking, talking too much

tall very high

tambourine a small thin drum which you tap with your hand. It has small metal discs around the edge which make a tinkling sound when you shake it.

tame not wild; able to live with human beings as pets, like tame rabbits

tamper to meddle or interfere with something

tan the brown color of your skin when you have been out in the sun for a long time. The same word also means to make animal hide into leather.

tangerine a kind of small sweet orange with a loose skin that comes off easily

tangled all twisted up in knots, like hair that has not been combed

tank a special heavy car made of iron and steel, with big guns in it. The same word also means a large metal or glass container for water and other liquids.

tanker a ship that carries oil or other liquids

tap to hit something lightly. The same word also means a kind of handle that you turn off and on to control the flow of something from a pipe, like gas and water.

tape a narrow strip of something such as strong cloth, plastic or sticky paper used to tie or fasten things together

tape recorder a machine that takes down and plays back sounds on a special kind of tape

tar a thick sticky black liquid which comes from wood and coal. Tar is used in making roads.

tardy late; slow

target something you aim at in shooting

tart a piece of pastry with jam or fruit in it

tartan a woolen material, especially worn in Scotland. It has a colored check pattern, and some Scottish families have their own special colors and patterns.

task a job; an amount of work that you have to do

tassel a number of threads all tied in a knot at the top. Tassels are used to decorate clothing or furniture.

taste to put a bit of food in your mouth or sip a drink to see if you like it or not

tax money paid to the government to help them pay for things we all use, such as roads, bridges, schools, hospitals and medicine

taxi a car that you pay to ride in

tea a hot drink made by pouring boiling water on to the dried leaves of the tea plant

teach to show someone how to do something; to give lessons

teacher someone who helps you to learn things

team a group of people all helping each other in a job or game

teapot a special pot to make tea in. It has a handle and a spout.

tear (*rhymes with spare*) to pull apart; to rip

tear (*rhymes with spear*) one of the drops of water that come from your eyes when you are sad or hurt

tease to annoy someone by making fun of him

teaser a tricky question or problem

teem to be abundant; to be full to overflowing as when a river teems with fish

teeth more than one tooth

telegram a short message sent by telegraph

telegraph a way to send messages quickly by electricity

telephone an instrument that carries your voice through electric wires so that you can speak to someone far away

telescope an instrument like a tube that you look through to see things that are far away, like the stars

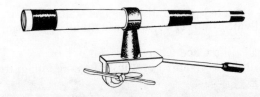

television   an instrument that brings pictures and sound through the air from far away

tell   to give news or say what you know about something

temper   the mood you are in. You can be in a bad temper and be cross with everyone, or in a good temper when you are nice to be with.

temperature   how hot or cold something is. It is measured in degrees.

tempest   a violent storm with a very strong wind

temple   a building in which people pray and worship

tempo   the speed (fast or slow) at which a piece of music should be played

tempt   to try to persuade someone to do something which he ought not to do

tender   soft; delicate. The same word also means gentle and loving.

tennis   a game played by two or four people. They use rackets to hit a ball back and forth over a net.

tent   a shelter made of a thick piece of cloth held up by strong sticks. You can camp out of doors under it.

tepee   a cone-shaped tent American Indians lived in

tepid   lukewarm

term   a limited period of time. The school year is divided into terms, with vacations between.

terminal   the place where buses, trains or airplanes end their journeys

terrace   a raised flat area of earth: a row of houses joined together

terrible   dreadful, awful

terrier   a kind of small dog

terrific   fearful, alarming. The same word can also be used to mean very great.

terrify   to frighten someone very greatly

terror   very great fear

test   an examination to find out how much someone knows. The same word also means to find out whether something such as a car or a machine is working properly.

tether   to tie an animal with a rope or chain so that it can walk around a bit, but cannot get away

thankful   grateful; pleased

thank you   You say *thank you* when someone has been kind or has given you something, and you want to show them you are pleased.

thatch   a roof or covering of straw or reeds

theater   a building where plays are acted

theft   the act of stealing

themselves   those people; they and no one else

therefore   for that reason

thermometer   an instrument for measuring how hot or cold something is

thick   wide or deep; the opposite of thin

thicket   shrubs and trees growing closely together

thief   someone who steals

thigh   the thick part of your leg above the knee

thimble   a metal or plastic cover for the top of your finger. It keeps the needle from hurting you when you are sewing.

thin   not wide or fat; the opposite of thick

thing   an object which is not named

think   to use your mind to help you do things better: to have ideas

third   next after second; one of three

thirsty   wanting to drink

thistle   a plant with a prickly stem and leaves. It grows wild and usually has purple flowers.

thorn   a sharp woody spike or prickle on a bush or shrub

thorough   complete; very careful

thou   an old-fashioned word for *you*

though   although

thought   an idea; something that is in your mind

thoughtful   thinking deeply: thinking of what others would like

thrash   to beat

thread   a very thin, very long piece of material used in sewing

threaten   to warn someone that you are going to punish or harm him

thresh   to beat out grain from its covering. Sometimes the word is spelled thrash.

thrill   a feeling of excitement

throat   the inside of the front of your neck which contains the gullet and the windpipe

throb   to quiver; to feel your heart beating strongly, as when you have been running very fast

throne   a special chair for a king or queen on ceremonial occasions

throttle   to choke or strangle. The same word also means the fuel control of a car engine.

through   from one end to the other

throughout   in every part

throw   to release something like a ball or a stone out of your hand and into the air with some force

thrush   a wild song bird with a brown and white speckled breast

thrust   to push with great force; to stab

thud   a heavy bumping sound when something falls to the ground

thumb   the short thick finger on your hand

thunder   the loud noise which you hear during a
storm after a flash of lightning

thus   therefore; in this way

tick   a soft clicking noise such as a clock
makes

ticket   a small piece of paper or cardboard which
you get when you pay to ride on a public
vehicle, or go to a show

tickle   a funny feeling on your skin which makes
you want to scratch. Sometimes it can
makes you laugh when someone tickles
you.

tide   the coming in and going out of the sea

tidy   neat; in order; not in a mess

tie   to make a knot with string or ribbon. The same
word also means a narrow piece of cloth worn
around the neck.

tiger   a dangerous wild animal like a very large cat.
It has striped fur, and lives mostly
in India.

tight   close-fitting; closely packed; the opposite of
loose

tighten   to make something tight or tighter

tile a flattish piece of baked clay which is used for roofs and sometimes for floors

till up to a certain time. The same word also means a special drawer where a shopkeeper keeps his money.

tilt to lean to one side

timber wood which is going to be made into something or used for building

time seconds, minutes, hours, days, weeks, months and years

timid easily frightened; the opposite of brave

tin a silvery metal. The same word also means a container made of tin.

tingle a prickly feeling

tinkle a small ringing sound

tinsel long strips of silvery sparkling material which are used to decorate Christmas trees

tiny very, very small

tip the thin end of something, usually pointed. The same word also means to overturn or tilt something.

tiptoe to walk on the tips of your toes very quietly

tire to become tired; to bore or make someone tired. The same word also means a rubber ring, usually filled with air, on the outer rim of the wheel of a car or bicycle.

tired When you are tired you have the feeling that you want to rest or go to sleep.

title   the name of something, such as a book, a song or a play. The same word also means a word in front of someone's name such as Sir, Lord, Doctor, or Captain.

toad   an animal that looks like a frog which has a rough, lumpy skin. It usually lives on land.

toadstool   a poisonous plant shaped like a mushroom

toast   bread which is made brown and crisp by heating it

tobacco   a plant with large leaves which are dried, cut up and used for smoking in cigarettes, cigars or a pipe

toboggan   a long flat sled curved up at the front, usually without runners

today   on this day

toddle   to walk with short wobbly steps like a very young child

toe   a part of your foot. You have five toes on each foot.

toffee   a sweet sticky food made from sugar and butter

together   being with

toil   to work very hard, with great effort

toilet   a lavatory. The same word also means washing, dressing and doing your hair.

tomato   a soft round red fruit, often used as a vegetable or in salads

tomb a place where someone is buried, either in the ground or in a stone box above the ground

tomboy a girl who behaves like a boy and enjoys playing boys' games

tomorrow the day after today

ton a measurement of weight. One short ton is equal to 2,000 pounds, and one long ton is equal to 2,400 pounds.

tone a sound, usually musical. The word is also used to describe the way a person's voice sounds, such as a harsh or sweet tone of voice.

tongue the thick soft part inside your mouth that moves when you talk and with which you taste things

tongs a tool with two pieces of metal like pincers for holding and lifting things

tonight this night

tonsil one of two little round pieces of flesh at the back of your mouth. Sometimes they have to be taken out if they become unhealthy.

too as well; also

tool any instrument that helps people to do work. Hammers and shovels are tools.

tooth one of the white bones in your mouth that you use to bite with

toothache a pain in your teeth

toothbrush a small long-handled brush which you use to clean your teeth

toothpaste a paste which you squeeze from a tube on to a toothbrush and use to clean your teeth

---

top the highest part of something. The same word also means a spinning toy.

topic any subject people choose to speak, write or argue about

torch a light which you can carry about, like an electric torch or a stick which is flaming at one end

torpedo a long rounded bomb which is fired through or along the surface of water

torrent a very fast-moving stream or river

tortoise a slow-moving animal with a very thick shell

torture to make someone suffer great pain, usually to make him confess or admit something

toss to throw something carelessly into the air

tot a small child

total the sum of; the whole amount

totter to walk unsteadily and shakily

touch to feel something with your fingers or with some part of your body

tough hard; strong; not easily broken

tour to travel round for pleasure from place to place, ending up where you started from

tournament a sports competition which several teams try to win, to see which is the best

tow (*rhymes with go*) to pull something by a rope

towards in the direction of

towel a piece of thick cloth or paper that you use to dry things that are wet

tower a building or part of a building that is very high and narrow

town a lot of houses and buildings together. It is larger than a village.

toy something children play with

trace to copy a drawing by putting transparent paper over it and going over the lines with a pencil

track a rail or set of rails upon which a train runs. The same word also means a mark, like a footprint, left by the passing of a person, animal or thing. The word also means a type of road.

tractor a heavy motor with wheels that pulls something along

trade to buy and sell: to exchange. The same word also means a particular kind of business, like hairdressing or dressmaking.

traffic cars, buses and vans moving along the streets

tragedy a disaster; a terribly sad happening

trail footprints or other signs that have been left by something or someone moving ahead of you

trailer any wheeled vehicle drawn behind a motor car or truck

train railroad cars pulled along a track by an engine. The same word also means to teach.

trainer   someone who teaches a person or animal to do something well, like swimming or running in a race

traitor   someone who betrays his friends or country

tramp   to walk heavily. The same word also means a person who wanders from place to place, often sleeping out of doors and begging for money from other people.

trample   to tread heavily on something

trampoline   a large piece of canvas fastened to a frame with springs. You can bounce up and down and do somersaults on it.

transfer   to carry or send something or someone from one place to another

transform   to change the way something looks, as a caterpillar is transformed into a butterfly

translate   to express the meaning of words in one language in another language

transparent   easily seen through. Window glass is transparent.

transplant   to remove a plant from the ground and plant it somewhere else. The same word also means a kind of surgery in which a diseased part of the body is removed and a healthy part put in its place.

transport   to carry something from one place to another

trap   a way of catching animals or birds

trapdoor   a door in the floor or ceiling

trapeze   a kind of swing with only
    a thin bar for a seat

travel   to make a journey; to go from place to place

trawler   a special fishing boat that drags a large net
    along the bottom of the sea

tray   a flat piece of wood, metal or plastic, on
    which you can carry light things, such as cups
    and saucers and food

treacherous   not to be trusted; likely to betray

tread   to step or walk

treasure   a collection of money or jewels. The
    same word also means anything which is
    valuable or much loved.

treat   to act in a certain way towards someone or
    something. The same word also means a
    special outing or present for which you do not
    have to pay.

tree   a very large plant with leaves and branches

tremble   to shake or shiver

tremendous   very large; enormous; huge

trench   a deep ditch

trespass   to go on someone else's land or property
    without permission

trial   a test to see if something works well: the
    judging of a person in a court of law

triangle   an area with three straight sides

tribe   a group of families who all live together with one chief who rules them

trick   something clever. Some people can do magic tricks and others can do tricks like walking on a wire, or standing on a horse when it is running.

trickle   to flow in a very small stream

tricycle   a three-wheeled cycle

trifle   something small and unimportant

trigger   the little lever which is pulled to fire a gun

trim   to make something neat, often by cutting off rough edges and loose threads. The same word also means to decorate a piece of clothing by adding lace, ribbons or some other pretty trimming.

trip   a short journey. The same word also means to stumble or fall as a result of catching your foot on something.

trot   to run, but not as fast as you can

trouble   anything which annoys or causes worry or unhappiness

troublesome   causing trouble or difficulty

trough   a long narrow container which holds water or food for animals

trousers a piece of clothing which covers you from your waist to your ankles, fitting around each leg separately

trout a kind of fish which lives in fresh water and is very good to eat

trowel a little spade with a curved blade. It is used in the garden for turning over earth and digging up small plants.

truck a big open vehicle for carrying heavy things from place to place

trudge to walk along wearily, with heavy footsteps

true real; correct

trumpet a musical instrument that you blow into

trunk the thick stem of a tree. The same word also means an elephant's nose, or a big box for sending clothes in.

trust to believe that someone is honest, or that you will not be tricked

truth whatever is true and has really happened

try to test to see if something works: to do the best you can

trying annoying; rather naughty

tub an open container for washing in or for holding liquids

tube a long thin hollow piece of metal, wood or other material. The same word also means a container from which you squeeze out the contents, such as toothpaste.

tuck to roll or fold up

tuft a small bunch of grass, hair or feathers, growing closely together

tug to pull hard at someone or something

tugboat a small but powerful ship which tows larger ships

tug of war a game in which a team pulls on each end of the same rope. Each team tries to pull the other team over a line.

tulip a brightly-colored flower with a few large leaves. It grows from a bulb.

tumble to fall over suddenly

tumbler a plain drinking glass with no stem

tummy a pet name for stomach

tune a lot of musical notes played one after the other to make a pretty sound

tunic a close-fitting jacket worn as part of a uniform. The same word also means a loose-fitting belted garment.

tuning-fork a metal instrument with two prongs that give out a musical sound when you strike it

tunnel a hole cut right through a hill or under the ground

turban a long piece of cloth wound round the head and worn as a hat

turbine an engine that works by force of water, steam or gas

turf the top layer of earth with grass growing on it

turkey   a big farmyard bird with
small wings and a fan-shaped tail

turn   to move yourself or some object to the left or
the right or all the way round

turning   a road branching off a main road to the left
or right

turnip   the large round root of the turnip plant
which can be cooked and eaten

turntable   the part of a record-player which goes
round and round when a record is played

turpentine   a kind of oil used in painting. It comes
from pine trees.

turret   a small tower on a building. The same word
also means a revolving platform on a ship or
tank that has guns on it.

turtle   an animal with a shell, like a tortoise. It has
paddle-shaped legs and lives in water.

tusk   one of the two very long teeth that stick out
of the mouths of some animals such as
elephants

tweed   a thick, rather rough woolen cloth which is
often used to make suits and overcoats

twice   two times

twig   a little branch on a tree or bush

twilight   the fading dim light just before the
sun sets

twin one of two children or animals born at the same time to the same mother

twine threads twisted together to make strong string. The same word also means to turn or twist round something.

twinkle to shine and sparkle in flashes, like a star in the sky

twirl to turn round and round very quickly

twist to bend something; to wind one thing around another; to turn sharply

twitter to make a chattering noise, as birds do when a lot of them are together

type to print words on paper by using a typewriter. The same word also means something that belongs to or stands for a group of things, like a type of person or type of food.

typewriter a machine which prints words on paper. It has keys with letters on them which you press.

tyrant a person who rules over people in a cruel way

ugly not pretty or pleasant to look at

ukelele a small musical instrument shaped like a guitar

ulcer   an open sore on the skin or inside you

umbrella   a round piece of material stretched over thin pieces of metal. It can be opened and held over your head to keep you from getting wet in the rain.

umpire   someone who settles arguments and decides whether players have broken the rules in games like baseball and tennis

uncle   the brother of your mother or father

uncomfortable   not at ease; feeling awkward

underground   underneath the ground

underline   to draw a line under a word

underneath   in a lower place; under something

understand   to know what something means

undo   to unfasten, untie or open something

undone   unfastened; opened

undress   to take your clothes off

unexpected   not expected; sudden

unfair   not fair or right

unhappy   not happy; sad

unhealthy   not healthy; sickly

unicorn   an imaginary animal that looks like a horse with a horn in the middle of its forehead

uniform   special clothes worn by those who belong to a group of people such as the army or the navy

unimportant   not important

uninteresting   not interesting

union   a joining together. The same word also means a group of workers who have joined together.

unit   a single thing

unite   to join together; to do something together as a group

universal   to do with everyone, everywhere

universe   all things existing on the earth and out in space

university   a place where students who have finished school can go for more education

unkind   not kind; cruel

unknown   not known; strange

unless   if not; if you do not

unlike   not like; different

unload   to take a load from; to take the bullets out of a gun

unpleasant   not pleasant; nasty

unsteady   not steady; shaky

unsuccessful   not successful; not able to do something you try to do

untidy   not neat; not well arranged

until   up to the time. You are not allowed to drive a car until you are old enough.

unusual   not usual; out of the ordinary

unwell   ill; not healthy

unwrap   to take the covering off something

up   towards a higher place; the opposite of down

upon   on top of something

uppercut   an upward blow used by a boxer

uproar   a noisy disturbance; shouting and yelling

upset   to knock something over. The same word also means to be worried or ill.

upside-down   turned over, with the top part underneath

upstairs   on a floor above the ground floor of a building

upstream   towards the upper part of a stream

upward   going up

urban   having to do with towns or cities and not the countryside

urge   to try to get someone to do something; to try to persuade

use   to do something with an object made for a special purpose. You use a knife to cut your food.

used   something that is not new

useful   something that is likely to be used a lot; helpful

useless   of no use; of no worth or value

usual   happening more often than not

usually   almost always; more often than not

vacant   empty; not lived in, like a house that people have moved away from

vacation   a holiday

vaccinate (*say vaksinate*)   to give an injection that will prevent you from getting some diseases

vacuum   a space with no air in it

vague   not very clear or sure

vain   thinking how pretty or good-looking you are; having a very good opinion of yourself

valentine   a card or greeting sent to someone you love on Saint Valentine's Day, February 14th

valley   the low land between two hills or mountains

valuable   worth a lot of money; high-priced: important

value   the worth of something; the price or cost of something

van   a closed motor vehicle used for carrying things from place to place

vane   a shaped piece of metal on top of a building, that swings to show which way the wind is blowing

vanilla   a food flavoring which comes from the dried seed pod of a climbing plant

vanish   to go out of sight very quickly; to disappear

vanity   too high an opinion of yourself

vapor   mist, steam or smoke floating in the air

variety   a collection of many kinds of things: a show with different kinds of entertainment

various   different; many; several. Ice cream comes in various flavors.

varnish   a clear liquid that you paint on to wood and metal to make it look shiny

vase   a pretty container for putting flowers in

vast   huge; very big; immense

veal   the meat from a calf

vegetable   any plant used for food

vehicle   any form of transport with wheels

veil   a thin piece of netting or material, worn by women to hide their faces or to protect them from strong wind or sunshine

vein   one of the very thin long tubes that carry the blood around in your body

velvet   soft warm material that looks and feels like very thin fur

vengeance   revenge

ventilator   a small opening in a wall to let stale air out or fresh air in

veranda   an open porch with a roof, joined on to a house. The word is also spelled verandah.

verse   poetry; part of a poem

vessel   a ship. The same word also means a
    container, usually for liquid.

vest   an undershirt; a waistcoat

vet   a person who looks after sick animals. The
    word is short for veterinary surgeon.

vex   to annoy someone or make him cross

viaduct   a long bridge made to carry a road or
    railway over a valley or low-lying area

vicious   wicked; fierce; very spiteful

victim   a person who is hurt in some way or is
    killed by someone else's action

victory   the winning of a battle or contest

videotape   a special kind of tape that shows pictures
    and gives out sounds when it is played through
    a special machine

view   what you can see in front of you. When you
    are on top of a hill, you have a good view
    of the countryside around
    the hill.

vigor   strength

viking   a pirate from the north in olden times

village   houses and buildings all together, like a
    town but smaller

villain   a bad man; a rogue

vine   a plant that climbs up poles or a fence or
    wall or creeps along on the ground. Some vines
    have grapes on them.

vinegar an acid-tasting liquid used in salads and pickles

violent very rough; forceful

violet a small wild plant with purple or white flowers

violin a musical instrument with four strings. It is held under the chin and played with a special stick called a bow.

visible able to be seen

visibility the clearness with which things can be seen. In a fog or mist the visibility is bad because you cannot see far.

vision the ability to see; eyesight

visit to go to see someone at his house

vitamin something in foods that is good for you because it keeps you healthy. Milk and oranges both have vitamins that you need.

vivid very bright; brilliant

vixen a female fox

vocabulary all the words you can speak and write: a selected list of words, usually in alphabetical order

voice the sound that comes from people's mouths when they speak or sing

volcano a cone-shaped mountain that throws out hot ashes or liquid rock from an opening in the top

volume a book. The same word also means the amount, quantity or bulk of something.

volunteer to offer to do something that you don't have to do

vote to say which person you would choose to be in charge of something or to be a member of a committee or similar group of people

vow a solemn promise

vowel the sounds of a language which are not consonants. Usually vowels are written with the letters *a e i o u.*

voyage a long journey by sea

vulgar rude; not very polite

vulture a large bird of prey that eats dead flesh

wad a bundle of paper, often used for packing

waddle to walk with short steps, rocking from side to side, as a duck does

wade to walk in water

wafer a very thin biscuit

wag to move something up and down or from side to side, as when a dog wags its tail

wage payment for a job of work

wagon an open vehicle with four wheels, used to carry heavy loads

wail to make a long sad crying noise

waist the narrow middle part of your body above the hips

waistcoat   a short sleeveless jacket, sometimes worn by men under a coat

wait   to stay in a place until someone comes or something happens

waiter   someone who serves food at a table in a café or restaurant

wake   to become awake after being asleep; to wake up someone who is asleep

walk   to move along on your feet, but more slowly than running

walkie-talkie   a radio carried about with you when you walk, used to send and receive messages

wall   something built of bricks or stone, like the sides of a house or a fence around a garden

wallet   a small pocket case, usually of leather, for carrying paper money, tickets, stamps and personal papers

wallop   to hit someone hard

wallpaper   a special kind of paper put on the inside walls of houses as decoration

walnut   a tree which has nuts that are good to eat. The wood is very hard, and is used to make furniture.

walrus   a sea animal, like a large seal with two tusks

wan   pale; looking rather ill or weak

wand   a magic stick used by fairies or by conjurers when they do magic tricks

wander   to roam about from place to place

wane   to become smaller, as when the full moon begins to wane

want   to wish for or to need something

war   a fight between two or more countries. If two groups of people in the same country fight each other, it is called civil war.

ward   a large room in a hospital, where there are a number of beds for sick people

warder   a man who stands guard over prisoners in a prison

wardrobe   a cupboard where you keep clothes

warehouse   a building where goods are stored

warm   more hot than cold

warn   to tell someone to take care because of something that may happen, usually dangerous

warp   to twist out of shape

warrior   a man who fights for his country in time of war; an old-fashioned word for soldier

warship   a ship that has guns and weapons for fighting in a war

wart   a small hard lump on the skin, usually on the hands or face

wash   to make clean, using soap and water

washing clothes that are being washed or need to be washed

wasp a stinging insect something like a bee with a very narrow waist

waste to use something up or spend money carelessly. The same word also means rubbish; something of no value that is thrown away.

watch to look at closely. The same word also means a small clock which you wear on your wrist or carry in your pocket.

watchful careful; watching what you are doing

water the clear liquid in lakes, rivers and seas. Water also falls from the clouds as rain.

watercress a green plant that grows in fresh water. It is eaten in salads and sandwiches.

waterfall a stream of water falling down from a high place

water lily a water plant with large flat floating leaves and beautiful pink, white or yellow flowers

watermelon a very large juicy fruit that grows on a creeping vine. It is dark green outside and red inside with lots of shiny dark brown seeds.

waterproof able to keep water out. A raincoat is waterproof.

wave water moving in a curved line on the surface of the sea or a lake. The same word also means to move something, like your hand or a flag, back and forth or up and down.

waver to sway; to falter; to be uncertain or undecided about what to do

wavy curving in and out

wax a soft yellowish material used in making candles. The same word also means sealing wax, which melts when you heat it, and then gets hard again.

way a road or path; space to move through. The same word also means how to do something, like the way to paint a picture.

wayfarer a traveler, especially one on foot

weak not strong

weaken to make something or someone weak

wealth great riches; a lot of money

wean to train a young child or young animal that has been living on milk to eat solid foods

weapon anything used to fight or hunt with, such as a gun, a heavy stick, or a bow and arrows

wear to be dressed in. You wear thin clothes in summer and thick clothes in winter.

weary very tired

weasel a small wild animal with a long slim body. It kills and eats other small animals.

weather what kind of day it is outside. The weather can be wet or dry, hot or cold.

weave to make cloth by twisting threads over and under each other

web the lacy net that spiders spin to trap insects

web-foot a foot that has skin joining the toes together. Ducks, geese and swans are all web-footed.

wedding the marriage ceremony, when a man and a woman become husband and wife

wedge a triangular piece of metal or wood, very thin at one end and thicker at the other. You put a wedge between two things to hold them firm or to push them apart.

wee small; tiny

weed wild plants that grow where they are not wanted in gardens or in fields where crops are grown

week seven days

weekend Saturday and Sunday

weep to cry tears

weigh to find out how heavy something is

weight the amount that something weighs

weird strange and frightening

welcome to greet someone with joy

well healthy; properly. The same word also means a deep hole in the ground from which oil or water is obtained.

west the direction in which the sun sets; the opposite direction to east

wet   not dry; covered with liquid

whack   to strike something so hard that it makes a noise

whale   the largest animal found in the sea

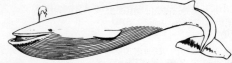

wharf   a landing place for loading and unloading ships

wheat   a kind of grain from which flour is made

wheel   a large flat circle made of wood or metal. Cars, buses and bicycles must have wheels to be able to move along.

wheelbarrow   a kind of small cart with only one wheel. You carry leaves and grass and building materials in it.

when   at what time; at the time that

whenever   at any time

where   at or in what place

whether   if or if not

whey   the watery part of milk. When cheese is made, the milk is separated into the thick part (called curds) and the liquid part (called whey).

which   one of two or more people or things, as when you decide which friend to invite or which flavor of ice cream you are going to have

whiff   a sudden puff of air, smoke, or scent

while   during the time that; as long as

whimper   to cry in a low whining voice

whine   to make a sad complaining crying sound

whinny   the noise a horse makes by blowing
through its nose

whip   a piece of thin strong cord or leather
attached to a handle. The same word
also means to stir up eggs or cream
very quickly.

whirl   to turn round and round very quickly

whisk   to move, sweep or stir something very
quickly

whisker   one of the stiff hairs on a man's face, or at
the sides of the mouths of some animals, such
as cats, lions and tigers

whiskey   a very strong drink made from grain

whisper   to speak so softly that only someone very
close to you can hear

whistle   to make a high musical sound by blowing
through your mouth with your lips nearly
closed. The same word also means a small
tube-like instrument that makes a whistling
sound when you blow it.

white   the color of snow

who   which or what person

whole   all; not a part; not divided

whoop   a loud cry or shout. The same word also
means the noise made by someone who has
the illness called whooping cough.

why   for what reason or cause, as *Why did you go away?*

wick   the twisted threads of cotton in a candle or lamp, which you light

wicked   evil; very bad; the opposite of good

wide   a long way from one side to the other; broad; the opposite of narrow

widespread   spread over a large space or among many people

widow   a woman whose husband is dead

widower   a man whose wife is dead

width   how wide or broad something is

wife   a married woman

wig   false hair that you put on over your own hair

wiggly   not straight, like this line   〰〰〰

wigwam   a tent or hut that American Indians lived in

wild   not kept or looked after by people; the opposite of tame

wilderness   a wild or desert area of land where no one lives

wildflower   a flower that grows without being planted by anyone

willful   wanting your own way

willing   pleased and ready to do something you are asked to do

willow   a tree with long bending branches and narrow leaves

wily   crafty, sly

win   to come first in something, like a race or a game

wind (*rhymes with tinned*)   fast-moving air that blows things about

wind (*rhymes with kind*)   to turn or twist something around, like winding up a ball of string

windmill   a machine that is worked by the wind. It is used for grinding grain or for pumping water.

window   a glass-covered opening in the wall of a building, which lets light and air in

wine   a strong drink made from the juice of grapes

wing   one of the two feathered parts of a bird's body with which it flies. Airplanes have metal wings.

wink   to shut and open one eye quickly

winter   the last of the four seasons of the year, when it is coldest

wipe   to clean or dry something by rubbing

wire   a very thin, long piece of metal

wireless   another name for radio, a way of sending sounds through the air without using wires

wise   knowing and understanding a lot of things

wish   to want something very much

wit   understanding, cleverness

witch   a wicked, dangerous woman who is supposed to be able to do magic

with   near to or alongside. Sometimes the same word also means against, as when you fight with someone.

wither   to dry up, to shrivel

within   inside; in the inner part

without   not having or using something. The same word also means on the outside.

witness   someone who has seen something happen and therefore can say he knows all about it

witty   clever and amusing

wizard   a man who is supposed to be able to do magic

wobble   to rock unsteadily from side to side

wolf   a dangerous wild animal, that looks like a large dog

woman   a female human being; a girl when she is grown up

wonder   to be surprised at something marvelous, unexpected or strange. The same word also means to question, to want to know.

wonderful   marvelous; amazing

wonderland   an imaginary country where amazing and wonderful things happen

wood   a little forest. The same word also means the material that trees are made of. Wood is used to make lots of things like fences, furniture and some buildings.

wooden   made of wood or hard like wood

woodpecker   a wild bird that pecks holes in the bark of trees to find insects for food

woodwork   carpentry; the wooden part of a building or furniture

wool   the thick warm covering of hair on a sheep, which is made into such things as blankets and clothing

woolen   made of wool

word   a spoken sound or group of letters that means something when you hear it or read it

work   to do something useful; not playing

works   a factory or workshop. The same word also means the machinery in something, such as a clock or watch.

world   the earth, the people and things on it, and the air around it

worm   a small snake-like animal which lives underground and moves by wriggling in the earth

worn looking shabby or ragged. Clothes look worn when you have been wearing them for a long time.

worry to be afraid something is going to go wrong or that something bad may happen to someone

worse not so good; more bad

worship to honor and praise God

worst most bad

worth the price you would have to pay for something you want to buy. The same word also means deserving or useful; good enough or valuable enough, as when someone says a book is worth reading.

worthless not worth anything; no good

wound (*rhymes with round*) turned and twisted

wound (*rhymes with spooned*) a cut in your flesh

wrap to cover something by folding paper or cloth around it. The same word also means a shawl or cape worn by girls and women.

wrath great anger

wreath a ring of flowers or leaves twisted together

wreck anything that has been ruined or destroyed, leaving only useless bits and pieces. Sometimes the word is short for shipwreck.

wren a very small brown wild bird

wrest to pull something away from someone by force

wrestle to struggle with someone to see who is stronger

wriggle   to move by twisting and turning

wring   to make water come out of something, like wet clothes, by twisting and squeezing

wringer   a machine with two rollers that wring the water out of wet washing

wrinkle   a small fold or crease in material, cloth, paper or the skin of old people

wrist   the thin part of your arm that joins on to your hand

write   to draw letters or words so that people can read them

writhe   to wriggle or twist about

writing   something you have written

wrong   not right; evil or wicked

x-ray   a special kind of photograph which shows doctors what the inside of your body looks like

xylophone   a set of narrow pieces of wood that make musical sounds when they are hit with wooden hammers

yacht (*rhymes with got*)   a kind of boat, usually with sails, used for racing or for pleasure

yak   a long-haired ox

yap   to bark sharply

yard   a space, usually closed in by buildings or a fence. The same word also means a measurement of 36 inches or 3 feet.

yarn   thread made from wool or cotton. The same word also means a story told by someone who has traveled a lot.

yawn   to open your mouth wide and breathe air in and out slowly, especially when you are sleepy or bored

year   a length of time; 365 days, 52 weeks or 12 months make a year

yearn   to wish very much for something

yell   to call out very loudly

yellow   a color. Lemons and dandelions are yellow and so are the yolks of eggs.

yelp   a short sharp cry or bark

yes   the word you use to show you agree

yesterday   the day before today

yet   by now. The same word sometimes also means but.

yield   to give up, as when the enemy surrenders. The same word also means to produce, as when a field of wheat yields a good crop.

yogurt   slightly sour thick milk, often mixed with a fruity flavoring. The word is sometimes spelled yoghurt or yoghourt.

yolk   the yellow part in the middle of an egg

yonder   over there; beyond

young   not old; in the early part of life

younger   not as old as someone else

youngster   a young person who is not yet grown up

yourself   you and no one else

youth   the time when you are young. The same
word also means a young man.

yo-yo   a toy in the shape of a reel, which spins up
and down on a string

zebra   a wild animal like a small horse with stripes

zero   nothing

zest   joy in what you are doing; enthusiasm

zigzag   moving from side to side, like this line

zinc   a bluish-white metal

zip   a long metal or plastic fastener used to do up
clothing and to close purses and bags

zipper   another word for zip-fastener

zither a musical instrument made of a flat board
with lots of metal strings stretched across it.
You pluck the strings to make musical sounds.

zone a large area of the world which is different
from other areas because, for example, it has a
much hotter or much colder climate

zoo a place where wild animals are kept and people
can come to look at them. The word is short
for zoological gardens.